THE ETERNAL CITY

ROME AND THE ORIGINS OF CATHOLIC CHRISTIANITY

TAYLOR R. MARSHALL, PH.D.

ORIGINS OF CATHOLIC CHRISTIANITY TRILOGY
VOLUME THREE

SAINT JOHN PRESS
MMXII

Sacred Scripture citations generally from the 1899 edition of the Douay-Rheims (Challoner) Bible, or based upon it.

Marshall, Taylor
The Eternal City:
Rome and Origins of Catholic Christianity / Taylor Marshall
1st ed.
Includes bibliographical references and index
ISBN: 978-0-9884425-0-4
1. Roman Catholicism 2. New Testament. 3. Theology. I. Title.

Published by
Saint John Press
PO Box 568011
Dallas, Texas 75365

Printed in the United States of America
Acid-free paper for permanence and durability
Covert Art: Steven M. Nelson {smnelsondesign.com}

Please visit *The Eternal City* on the web at:

www.taylormarshall.com

Dedicated to my beloved children. I love you all dearly. I pray for you daily. Please pray for me—and please remember me at the altar after I die.

> Behold the inheritance of the Lord are children: the reward, the fruit of the womb. As arrows in the hand of the mighty, so the children of them that have been shaken. Blessed is the man that hath filled the desire with them; he shall not be confounded when he shall speak to his enemies in the gate.
>
> Psalm 126, D-R

As long as the Coliseum stands,
Rome shall stand.
When the Coliseum falls,
Rome will fall.
When Rome falls,
the world will fall.

Saint Bede the Venerable
A.D. 673–735

And both the city and her lands, in truth
were established as the place of holiness
where the successors of great Peter sit.

Dante Alighieri
Inferno II, 22-24

CONTENTS

ACKNOWLEDGEMENTS

I must chiefly acknowledge my beloved spouse for her constant encouragement and love. **Joy** is truly my joy. I am also grateful for my children who remind me of the reasons for which I write.

My thanks are due to all of my professors, teachers and mentors.

Charles Page edited the manuscript beautifully. His hand is on every page. **Jonathan Deane** also made excellent last-minute additions. This book would not be what it is without him. Thank you Charles. **Steven Nelson** did a wonderful job creating the cover art for this book and the previous two volumes of the *Origins of Catholicism* trilogy.

A special thanks to **John Boyden** who was my very first Catholic guide to the Eternal City in 2006. Many of the things he showed me found their way into this book.

My thanks are also due to **Bishop James Conley, Bishop Kevin Vann, Scott Hahn, Dave Palmer** at Guadalupe Radio, **Matthew Swaim, Brent Stubbs, Matthew Levering, Jordan Low, Daniel & Bettina Hennessy, Jared Goff, Joseph Reidy, Albert Doskey, Marcus Grodi, Christina Mehaffey** and all my friends at Faustina Academy, **Kevin Knight** at newadvent.org, **Tito Edwards** at thepulp.it, **Father James Lehrberger, O.Cist.,** and **Christopher Malloy** at the University of Dallas.

I would like to thank **Father Phil Wolfe, FSSP, Father Juan Diego, CFR, Father Paul Check,** and **Father Gary Selin.**

My honor and gratitude are due to my loving and supportive parents **William** and **Jennifer**.

HOW I FOUND SAINT PETER

February 2. Feast Day of the Purification of Mary. I was still an Episcopalian priest. My wife Joy was pregnant with our fourth child. We traveled to Rome with a question that had been pricking our consciences: "Is the Catholic Church the *true* Church of our Lord Jesus Christ?"

If you have read the first book in the trilogy, *The Crucified Rabbi*, you read about my encounter with the Rabbi at the hospital and my theological inquiry into Catholicism. After prayer and late night conversations, Joy and I were ready. We had flown to Rome, and we were ready to seal the deal.

That day, we got in line for the Vatican *Scavi* Tour. This tour leads pilgrims through the narrow passages beneath the floors of Saint Peter's Basilica into the long lost inner sanctum of the basilica. Here in the darkness, below the feet of those in the church is the first century burial plot of Saint Peter.

Our tour guide was a priest from Belgium who spoke excellent English. Joy and I were, by far, the most enthusiastic members of that morning's tour group. At the end of the tour, we at last came to the Tropaion, which had been built over Peter's tomb, and there we saw the bones of Saint Peter.

I was not then a Catholic. However, the weight of sanctity in that place pushed me to my knees. I knelt down, and I prayed to Saint Peter. "Holy Peter, I'm ready. Please lead me into communion with your successor, the Vicar of Jesus Christ my Lord."

After the tour, the Belgian priest stayed behind and struck up a conversation with us. We seemed so excited and impressed by the tour that he wanted to know who we were. When I told him that we were not Catholics, but that I was an Episcopalian priest, his face lit up. He was writing his dissertation in Rome on some ecumenical matter. Then he surprised us with a question: "Would you like to attend Holy Mass with the Pope this evening?"

The answer to that question was obvious. The Belgian priest was pleased to make arrangements. We walked from the *Scavi* entrance on the south side of Saint Peter's, across Saint Peter's Square, and then up a staircase to the north. At the top were two Swiss Guards with pikes. The Belgian priest told us to wait there. He mumbled some Italian to the guards and disappeared.

A few minutes later he returned with two orange tickets, which were marked with that evening's date and were issued by the Palazzo Apostolico Vaticano. The Belgian priest told us to return to Saint Peter's an hour before the Mass with those tickets. We had a nice chat, and the priest went about his business. To my shame, I don't know his name.

That evening, my wife and I attended the Holy Mass of the Purification. At this particular Holy Mass the Holy Father recognized the various religious orders of the world. We were in line with hundreds of nuns, friars, and monks. We were clearly out of place—a married Episcopalian priest in a cassock with a pregnant wife. My dear! I hope we did not scandalize all those nuns.

The Holy Mass was glorious. It began in total darkness. Pope Benedict XVI entered the back doors with only a candle. From this candle was lit all the candles of the nuns, monks, and friars. For the whole Mass, we were near the bronze statue of Saint Peter. I could see the Holy Father clearly. I knew that His Holiness was the true successor of the Fisherman, and recalling that just that morning I had been deep underneath that altar at the bones of Saint Peter, the connection between the ministry of Saint Peter the First Pope and that of Benedict XVI the present Pope was made manifest right before my eyes.

When it came time for Holy Communion, I knew that I could not go forward to receive. I was not a Catholic. I was not in communion with the Holy Father. *I was in schism.* It was a sickening feeling. I was out of communion with the Vicar of Christ, and I knew in that moment that my relationship with Christ was impaired. I also knew what I had to do. I had to resign the Episcopalian priesthood and become a Catholic.

That next morning in Rome, I met with an impressive priest by the name of Monsignor James Conley at Saint Anne's Gate outside the Vatican. I had met Monsignor Conley the previous day after having met the Belgian priest. Monsignor Conley, over a strong cappuccino, had within a matter of minutes placed me into a theological headlock. Our conversation had been swift and covered topics such as Cardinal Newman's arguments against Anglicanism, Pope Leo XIII's *Apostolicae Curae*, the significance of *Dominus Jesus* in 2000, and Cardinal Ratzinger's clarification about Anglican Orders. Monsignor Conley was sharp, and he did not pull punches.

Monsignor Conley had arranged for me to meet with William Cardinal Baum. It was February 3—Feast Day of Saint Blaise. Monsignor Conley silently indicated that I was to go alone. Joy gracefully understood and perused the local stores. Meanwhile, I was escorted into a closed room overlooking Saint Peter's Square. The Cardinal entered the room, and we engaged in some small talk. I told him how we had attended Holy Mass with the Holy Father the evening before. His Eminence then initiated a theological investigation. "What do you believe about the Church? What do you believe about the sacraments? What do you believe about the Eucharist? What do you believe about Mary?" His questions seemed endless, and tried to answer to the best of my ability.

At the end of this unexpected oral examination, Cardinal Baum leaned back in his chair, closed his eyes, and said, "My son, you are a Catholic. You must come home." This was a great moment of clarity. We spoke about the next steps. After an hour or so, I asked for his blessing. His Eminence gave me a beautiful blessing in Latin—for me and for my family. We then entered his private chapel and prayed together—a *Pater Noster*, an *Ave Maria*, and a *Gloria Patri* in Latin. His Eminence left me with kind words and sent me on my way. He knew that I would soon be a Catholic. When Joy and I arrived back in Texas, I notified Bishop Kevin Vann right away. He graciously met with me and received us into the Catholic Church. We had finally come home, but our journey had just begun.

But Why Rome?

Before we entered the Catholic Church, we Episcopalians used to balk at the claims of the *Roman* Catholic Church. Episcopalians, also known as Anglicans, derive from the Church of England, which was established by King Henry VIII in his desire to obtain an annulment for his valid marriage with Queen Catherine of Aragon. The word "Anglican" derives from the Latin word *Anglicanus* mean "English." Because the Catholic Church refused to grant King Henry an annulment, he broke from Rome in 1534.

Everyone knows that King Henry's adultery and his subsequent desire for annulment was a lousy justification for ecclesiastical schism. No Episcopalian or Anglican can honestly appeal to King Henry VIII as a saintly or pious king with right intentions. Henry VIII didn't create the Anglican Church out of profound devotion to the Lord Jesus Christ. Rather, everyone admits that Henry was a politically ambitious tyrant.

Catholics often ask me, "Taylor, you used to be an Anglican. How can Anglicans justify their existence? Technically they belong to a church that was founded by a rascal wearing a crown."

We Episcopalians or Anglicans had a very clever answer to this objection. Yes, we granted that Henry VIII had bad intentions, and we carefully distanced ourselves from his reputation. To answer the common objection, we simply claimed that while we were not *Roman Catholic*, we were nevertheless still *Catholic*. We claimed to be *Anglo-Catholics,* that is, Catholics of merry old *Æng*land. Allow me to explain.

The Catholic Church in England is as ancient as the third century at the latest. One tradition holds that disciples of Saint John evangelized Britannia. Another tradition holds that Saint Linus, the second Pope after Saint Peter, was the son of a British king, one Caratacus. Yet another tradition holds that Christianity was carried to England by Saint Joseph of Arimathea.

Citing these traditions, we Anglicans claimed that Christianity in England has deep roots predating "Roman interference." It was not until A.D. 664 at the Synod of Whitby, we Anglicans claimed, that the Anglo-Saxons officially expressed their submission and allegiance to the Pope in Rome. Yet by the sixteenth century, King Henry VIII, in his desire to obtain an annulment from his wife Queen Catherine of Aragon, severed his relationship with Rome and established himself as the Protector and Supreme Head over the Church of England.

This historical narrative allowed us to dismiss the claims of Rome to be the one and only Catholic Church. England had been perfectly Christian before it submitted to the Pope, and it could be perfectly

Christian without the Pope. For English Christianity, the Pope was optional—or so we thought. We Anglicans claimed to be Catholic, but not Italianate. This allowed us to use the word *Catholic* without blushing. Yes, Henry VIII was a tyrant, but we still retained our *Anglo-Catholicism* from a previous age. All this assumed, of course, that Rome and the Pope had nothing to do with being Catholic—an unfounded assumption as this present book shall demonstrate.

According to Anglicans and other Protestants, the central role of Rome in Christendom was merely an accident of history. There was, they claim, no theological significance for the primacy of Rome. Rather, Rome held preeminence since it was the imperial capital of the empire. With the fall of Rome and the globalization of the Church, Rome need not be the capital of Christianity. Why couldn't Constantinople, Moscow, or even New York be the capital of Christianity?

This line of reasoning once persuaded me. As I read the Old and New Testaments, it seemed that if any city on earth should be the capital of Christianity, it would have been Jerusalem. Jerusalem was thought to be the burial site of Adam. Jerusalem is the location of Mount Moriah, which was the place where Abraham nearly sacrificed Isaac (2 Chron 3:1). Jerusalem was the capital city of King David. Jerusalem is the place of Solomon's Temple and the topic of the prophets' warnings. Most notably, Jerusalem was the place of Christ's last supper, death, resurrection, ascension, and the descent of the Holy Ghost on Pentecost. Jerusalem, it would seem, is *the* place of God's activity. Why would Christ our Lord choose the pagan city of Rome?

As I studied the claims of Catholicism, I eventually came to assent to the theology of *Roman* Catholicism. However, I was still not clear on why the Bishop of Rome and the Holy See of Rome retained divine and supreme authority. Yes, I well understood that our Lord Jesus Christ, as King of Heaven and earth appointed Simon Peter as the Rock on which He would build His Church. Petrine authority was biblical. But did not Peter originally lead the Holy Apostles in Jerusalem, beginning with the descent of the Holy Ghost on Pentecost? Moreover, does not the universal tradition of the Church hold that Saint Peter was also Bishop of Antioch? If Saint Peter led Jerusalem and Antioch, why would Rome be the mother and mistress of all other churches?

I began to find my answer in two places. To my surprise, I found that the preeminence of Rome in the Kingdom of God was foretold in the Old Testament. Secondly, my visit to the *Scavi* tour beneath the floors of Saint Peter's Basilica in Rome opened my eyes to spiritual significance of Saint Peter's martyrdom. This book begins in the Old Testament and traces the biblical and theological significance of Rome as the necessary hub of redemptive history in the New Covenant. Rome, as the reader shall discover, is not the Holy and Apostolic See through an accident of imperial history. Rome is the center of God's earthly reign because it was chosen to be so from before the foundation of the world as foretold by the Hebrew prophets.

1. DANIEL FORETELLS THE ROMAN CHURCH

When therefore you shall see the abomination of desolation, which was spoken of by Daniel the prophet, standing in the holy place: he that readeth let him understand.

- Our Lord Jesus Christ
St Matthew 24:15

Before we get to Daniel, we need to see where his story fits into the big picture. The story of the Bible goes like this. God created all things. He made man and woman in his own image and likeness. Through the agency of Satan, man and woman fell from their original state of righteousness. However, God promised that the "seed of the woman" would strike the head of Satan and bring about a reversal of the curse of sin (Gen 3:15). The seed is a poetic term describing a child or heir.

Around 2,000 B.C. God chose a man named Abram and called him out of Babylonia. In the twelfth chapter of Genesis, God promised Abram three things: 1) a Promised Seed or Heir of Blessing; 2) a Promised Land; and 3) the Universal Blessing to All Nations (Gen 12:1-3). Next, God changed his name from Abram meaning "Exalted Father" to Abraham meaning, "Father of a Multitude". This threefold promise is the Abrahamic Covenant. God established circumcision as sign of his covenant with Abraham. In a certain sense, circumcision pointed toward the seed or future biological heir of the promise. God promised that this covenant would one day, "bless all the families of the earth."

Abraham never fully possessed the promise land, but he and his wife Sarah did conceive a promised child in their old age. His name was Isaac. Isaac in turn was the father of Jacob who wrestled with God and consequently received the name *Israel ("He-Who-Wrestles-God")*. Israel had twelve sons for whom the Twelve Tribes of Israel were named.[1] When the Promised Land experienced a severe famine, these twelve sons of Israel went to Egypt and prospered there until a new Pharaoh arose to the throne of Egypt. This Pharaoh enslaved the Israelites.

The Israelites remembered that they were supposed to be the great heirs of Abraham and possess the Promised Land. Instead, the Israelites had become slaves in Egypt. God heard their prayers and raised up a prophet around the year 1,490 B.C. His name was Moses, and God commissioned him by speaking to him through a burning bush.

Moses went before the Pharaoh, repeatedly proclaiming the command of God: "Let my people go!" Pharaoh hardened his heart, and so God brought through Moses ten terrible plagues. The final plague was the death of the firstborn son. Through Moses, God instructed the Israelites to keep the first Passover meal so as to exempt themselves from this final plague against the firstborn sons of Egypt. In the morning, having lost his firstborn son, the troubled Pharaoh told them to get out. The Israelites packed up and left Egypt, but before they had exited the borders of Egypt, the Pharaoh had a change of mind. Trapped between the Red Sea on one side and the Pharaoh on the other side, God miraculously opened the Red Sea and the Israelites escaped. This is the *Exodus*.

Once the Israelites were safely in the wilderness of Sinai, Moses ascended Mount Sinai to receive the Ten Commandments. While Moses was on Mount Sinai, the Israelites rebelled against God by crafting a golden calf with which they committed idolatry. In response to Israel's infidelity, God cursed Israel to roam the wilderness for forty years. At Mount Sinai (Exodus-Leviticus) and then later in Moab (Deuteronomy), Moses mediates a covenant of probation for the newly redeemed, but idolatrous, Israelites. This covenant mediated by Moses is the Mosaic Covenant.

The Mosaic Covenant consisted of 613 laws that established the moral, ceremonial, and civic code of Israel. The Mosaic Law prescribed the *kosher* food laws, described the construction of the Ark of the Covenant that housed the tablets of the Ten Commandments, and established the system of animal sacrifice at the tabernacle that functioned as a moveable cloth Temple.

At the end of the forty years of roaming in the wilderness, Moses appointed his successor Joshua to lead the next generation of Israelites into the Promised Land. Moses died, and tradition holds that an angel hid his body. Joshua led the Israelites across the Jordan River and into the Promised Land that had been promised to Abraham. They began to conquer the seven Canaanite nations that lived there previously, who were known for their idolatry, child sacrifice, and sexual immorality.

The Israelites battled these Canaanite peoples for hundreds of years. In about 1,020 B.C. God chose a shepherd boy named David to establish a permanent monarchy for Israel. In his love for God, David expressed his desire to build a permanent house of worship for God. In response to David's faithful love, God established David as the anointed king of Israel. God made three promises in this Davidic covenant in 2 Samuel 7:9-16. First, David's son would build a house for God's name, that is, God's permanent Temple (7:13). Second, God would establish the throne of his kingdom *for ever* (7:13, 16). Third, God would be his father, and David would be His son. (7:14). Thus, King David and his royal line of descendents became known by the title *Messiah*, meaning *Anointed One*.

King David chose the city of Jerusalem as his capital. He ruled from Jerusalem, and God revealed to him plans to build a permanent Temple in Jerusalem that would replace the cloth Tabernacle that housed the Ark of the Covenant. During the time of Solomon, the Israelites completely conquered and possessed the entire Promised Land.

This was the Golden Age of Israel with a united kingdom under David's son Solomon, a glorious Temple, and a fully possessed Promised Land. One thousand years had elapsed since God first made his promise to Abraham. At last, Abrahamic Covenant had *finally* come to fulfillment: the Seed (the Davidic Messianic lineage), secondly the Land (the conquered Promised Land), and thirdly the Universal Blessing to All Nations. Recall that Solomon consecrated the Temple as a house of prayer for all nations.

Then it all fell apart. God had appointed Israel to be a holy nation set aside to bless all the nations. Yet Israel did not fulfill this vocation. Just as Israel began to have international influence, King Solomon "the Wise" allowed idolatry to flourish in the land Israel. After Solomon died, Israel fell into civil war, and the ten northern tribes of Israel revolted against Solomon's heir in Jerusalem. These ten northern tribes established their own monarchy in the city of Samaria and built two new idolatrous temples in the north for worship of the golden calves—revealing that Israel's affection for "holy cows" had not yet been eradicated.

This division of Israel after the death of Solomon led to the establishment of two kingdoms. There was the Northern Kingdom of Israel with its capital in Samaria and the Southern Kingdom of Judah with its capital in Jerusalem. The Northern Kingdom was *de facto* idolatrous and God chastised the Northern Kingdom of Israel by sending them into exile under the Assyrians in 722 B.C. These northern Israelites were mingled with the nations and lost. They are the so-called "ten lost tribes" of Israel.

The Southern Kingdom of Judah was more faithful to God, but they also succumbed to idolatry. God led them into exile under the Babylonians in 587 B.C. This era is known as the Babylonian Exile. The Israelites of the Southern Kingdom of Judah became known as *Jews* since they belonged to the tribe of *Judah*. Incidentally, the word *Judaism* derives from this usage.

The Babylonian Exile was a bleak era in the history of redemption, but God had not abandoned the children of Abraham. God sent prophets who reassured his people of God's covenants to Abraham, Moses, and David. The message of the prophets announced that God would bring about redemption through the Promised Seed or descendent of Abraham and David— the Messiah. The Messiah would restore them in the Land and bring about the universal blessing to all nations.

During this era of exile in Babylon, God established a prophet named Daniel. Recognizing the inherent talents in Daniel, the Babylonians chose the astute young man to be servant of King Nebuchadnezzar of Babylon. Daniel was the King's good servant, but God's first. He faithfully served King Nebuchadnezzar but also religiously observed the Law of Moses. Instead of eating the sumptuous food of the king's table, he consumed only water and vegetables, because it was certain that the king's food was not prepared according to the kosher laws given by Moses.

The Four Kingdoms in Detail

It is in the prophecies of Daniel and the other prophets that we begin to see God preparing the world for the coming of the Messiah. Daniel describes two different visions that reveal a succession of four earthly kingdoms climaxing in the advent of God's Messianic Kingdom of Heaven. Daniel's prophecies foretell that there would be four Gentile (non-Jewish) kingdoms that will reign over the Jewish people until the coming of the Messiah and the restoration of the Kingdom of God.

The first vision is found in the second chapter of Daniel. It describes a dream of Nebuchadnezzar about an enormous statue composed of four different materials. First, the head was of gold. Second, the chest and arms were of silver. Third, the belly and thighs were of bronze. Fourth, the legs and feet were of iron and clay. According to the vision, a stone will be hewn from a mountain without human hands and cast into the statue. This small rock smashes against the statue's iron and clay feet, which causes the entire statue to crumble. Then the small rock becomes a great mountain and fills the entire earth.

Daniel interpreted the dream in the following way. First, the golden head was Nebuchadnezzar and his Babylonian Empire. Next, an inferior kingdom would then follow the Babylonian Empire, as silver is inferior to gold. Then, a third kingdom would arise inferior to the second kingdom, as bronze is inferior to silver. Lastly a fourth kingdom would arise that was different than the previous three. As for the small uncut rock cast down from Heaven, Daniel explains:

> And in the days of those kings, *the God of heaven will set up a kingdom that shall never be destroyed*, nor shall its sovereignty be left to another people. It shall break in pieces all these kingdoms and bring them to an end,

and *it shall stand forever*, just as you saw that *a stone* was cut from a mountain by no human hand, and that it broke in pieces the iron, the bronze, the clay, the silver, and the gold. A great God has made known to the king what shall be hereafter. The dream is certain, and its interpretation sure (Dan 2:44-45).

The stone from Heaven in the days of the Fourth Kingdom signifies that "the God of heaven will set up a kingdom that shall never be destroyed."

Looking in back in time, we understand the prophecy as corresponding to the following historical chronology when heathen kingdoms ruled over the Jews:

1. Babylonian Empire (ca. 587-539 B.C.)
2. Medo-Persian Empire (ca. 539-331 B.C.)
3. Greek Empire (ca. 331-168 B.C.)
4. Roman Empire (ca. 63 B.C.-A.D. 70)

It was in fact in the days of the Fourth Kingdom, the Roman Empire that God established His Messianic Kingdom:

In those days a decree went out from Caesar Augustus that all the world should be enrolled...And Joseph also went up from Galilee, from the city of Nazareth, to Judea, to the city of David, which is called Bethlehem, because he was of the house and lineage of David, to be enrolled with Mary, his betrothed, who was with child. And while they were there, the time came for her to be delivered (Lk 2:1-6).

It is also common knowledge that Christ was crucified under Pontius Pilate, the Roman governor of Judea. From a historical point of view we see that the Rock of Ages came crashing into the Roman Empire. The Kingdom of Christ began precisely when Daniel predicted—during the era of the Fourth Kingdom, the Kingdom of Rome.

Before moving on, it is important to note here that the Four Kingdoms of the Gentiles also began to anticipate a Messiah in their own way. Ezekiel and Daniel called King Nebuchadnezzar of Babylon "the King of Kings" (Ezek 26:7; Daniel 2:37), a title given subsequently to Jesus Christ. Isaiah called King Cyrus of Persia "the Messiah" (Isaiah 45:1), a surprising use of the term for a Gentile king! Alexander the Great of Greece united the Mediterranean world, had himself proclaimed the "Son of God," and died at the age of thirty-three. The Greco-Syrian ruler Antiochus IV later ruled the Promised Land, desecrated the Temple, and in turn became a type of the False Messiah or Antichrist.

The Fourth Beast and the Son of Man

In the seventh chapter of Daniel, the prophet records a related dream that he experienced concerning Four Beasts coming from the Great Sea. He sees:

1. a lion with eagle wings (Dan 7:4)
2. a bear raised up on one side with three ribs between its teeth (Dan 7:5)
3. a leopard with four wings and four heads (Dan 7:6)
4. a fourth beast, terrible and dreadful and exceedingly strong; and it had great iron teeth; it devoured and broke in pieces, and stamped the residue with its feet. It was

different from all the beasts that were before it; and it had ten horns (Dan 7:7).

The winged lion or *lamassu* is a common Babylonian motif and stands for the Babylonian Empire. The bear "raised up on one side" is the Medo-Persian Empire, within which the Persian part was stronger and exalted. The three ribs in the bear's mouth represent that the Medo-Persian Empire was able to put down the alliance of Egypt, Lydia, and Babylon.

The four-headed and four-winged leopard stands for the Greek Empire, which under the reign of Alexander the Great experienced rapid expanse. The four heads represent the four generals who divided the empire into four provinces after Alexander's death in 323 B.C. These four provinces were Macedonia, Asia Minor, Egypt, and Syria.

The fourth beast is not depicted as an animal, but as something "terrible and dreadful." Its "iron teeth" recall the "iron" Fourth Kingdom of the dream in the second chapter of Daniel. In fact, Daniel writes, "The fourth beast shall be a fourth kingdom upon the earth" (Daniel 7:23).

As in the vision of the second chapter of Daniel, God intervenes supernaturally during the kingdom of the Fourth Beast:

> I saw in the night visions, and behold, with the clouds of heaven there came one like the Son of Man, and he came to the Ancient of Days and was presented before him.
> And to him was given dominion and glory and kingdom,
> that all peoples, nations, and languages should serve him; his dominion is an everlasting dominion, which shall not pass

away, and his kingdom one that shall not be destroyed (Daniel 7:13-14).

This vision of the Son of Man coming on the clouds is a vision of the Messiah, and Jesus Christ identifies the vision as a description of Himself just before the Jewish and Roman authorities condemn Him:

> Jesus said to him, "You have said so. But I tell you, hereafter you will see the Son of Man seated at the right hand of Power, and coming on the clouds of heaven" (Mt 26:64).

Once again we find that Daniel rightly prophesies that the Messiah will arise in the time of the Fourth Kingdom. It is during the time of the Fourth Kingdom that the Messiah shall receive His own Kingdom—the Kingdom of God.

Daniel states that the Fourth Kingdom of Rome will "persecute the saints" (Daniel 7:25), and history testifies that Rome certainly persecuted not only Christ but also the early Church. Next, Daniel explains:

> [The Fourth Beast's] dominion shall be taken away, to be consumed and destroyed to the end. And *the kingdom* and the dominion and the greatness of the kingdoms under the whole heaven *shall be given to the people of the saints of the Most High;* their kingdom shall be an everlasting kingdom, and all dominions shall serve and obey them (Dan 7:26-27, emphasis added).

The kingdom is taken away from the Fourth Beast and given to whom? The last four lines leap off the page. Read them over and over again. Who receives the kingdom? *The people of the saints of the Most High!* The four kingdoms culminate in the coming of the Messiah, and then the kingdoms are given over to the saints of the Most High. The Lord Jesus Christ is the true King of Kings, the true Messiah, the true Son of God, and the true ruler of all the nations. The culmination of Daniel's Four Kingdoms—the Roman Empire—is handed over to people of Jesus Christ. The Church is *not* the Roman Empire, but it *receives* the Roman Empire. Daniel spoke of this before the coming of Christ, and the recorded history after Christ bears witness to this truth.

So as the Jews entered the age of the Fourth Kingdom of Rome, they desperately expected a Messiah. Meanwhile, the Gentile rulers posed vainly as quasi-Messianic demigods. As we shall see, first century Rome was an era of the most blasphemous and vile emperors in the history of mankind. However, before examining the horrors of first century Rome, let us examine Rome's first encounter with the nation of the Jews as it relates to the Festival of Lights—Hanukkah.

NOTES

[1] Two tribes, Ephraim and Manasseh, were named after Jacob's grandsons.

2. HANUKKAH AND THE JEWISH-ROMAN ALLIANCE

Good success be to the Romans and to the people of the Jews by sea, and by land, for ever: and far be the sword and enemy from them.

- 1 Maccabees 8:23

UNDER MEDO-PERSIAN RULE (539-331 B.C.), the Jews lived with relative freedom and were encouraged to practice their customs and faith. Under the Persian king Cyrus the Great, the Jews were even allowed to return to the Holy Land and rebuild the Temple in 515 B.C. Jewish life was not perfect, but it was tolerable under the Persians. Unfortunately, a young Macedonian warrior was going to bring all of this to an end. His name was Alexander—Alexander the Great.

Jews under the Third Kingdom of Greece

Alexander's father, Philip the Macedonian, had united the historically divided city-states of Greece into one powerful empire, but his son Alexander had more ambitious plans. Alexander expanded his father's project to encompass nearly the entire known world.

In the year 331 B.C. Alexander the Great conquered Daniel's Second Kingdom, the Medo-Persian Empire. Since Jerusalem remained under the dominion of Persia, it then fell under the rule of Alexander's Greek Empire. To the Jews it must have seemed that overnight it was no longer the Persians but the Greeks reigning over them. These Greeks would prove to be much less tolerant toward the monotheistic convictions of the Jewish people as the Persians had been.

The Greeks believed that a united empire required a united culture. They were convinced that unity required uniformity. Thus, the Greeks were keen to spread not only their language but also their culture to every region of the empire. The spread of Greek customs to the world is called *Hellenization*. The term derives from the name *Hellen*, the Greeks' traditional self-identified ethnicity, and refers to the process of ensuring that conquered cultures assimilated into the established Greek culture. Greek architecture, sculpture, poetry, philosophy, and religion flourished throughout Alexander's conquered territories. Greek became the language of literature, commerce, and politics.

Alexander the Great caught a terrible illness and died of a fever in 323 B.C. at the age of thirty-three. After his death there arose a long struggle for power until 281 B.C. when the Hellenistic Empire was formally divided into four Hellenized territories: Egypt, Syria, Macedonia, and Asia Minor. These four territories are the four heads of the four-headed leopard of Daniel's Third Kingdom (Dan 7:6).

The Bible Becomes International

Ptolemy I Soter who reined over the Egyptian quadrant resettled many Jews in the capital city of Alexandria. Under his successor Ptolemy II Philadelphus, the Hebrew Scriptures were translated into Greek. The translation of the Hebrew Scriptures into the Greek language was a major milestone in the history of the Bible. The Jewish people have always held their Hebrew Scriptures in great esteem. The fact that Hellenization incorporated even the Hebrew Scriptures testifies to the great success of Greek culture even within the culturally resistant Jewish community.

According to tradition, seventy-two Jewish scholars translated the Hebrew Scriptures into Greek. Philo of Alexandria relates that Ptolemy II Philadelphus desired a Greek version of the Hebrew Scriptures for the world famous Library of Alexandria. Seventy-two Jewish scholars were chosen and isolated into seventy-two separate chambers. Seventy-two days later, the seventy-two Jewish scholars emerged, each with their own independent Greek translation of the Hebrew text. Philo records that by a divine miracle, each of the seventy-two translations was identical to the others. In other words, the seventy-two scribes miraculously translated each and every word of the Hebrew Scriptures in exactly same way. Thus, this Greek version of the Hebrew Scriptures is known as the Septuagint, deriving from the Latin: *septuaginta interpretum versio* ("the version translated by the seventy"). It is commonly denoted with the Roman numeral for seventy: *LXX*.

The Greek Septuagint became very important for the early Christians. Greek was the language of the first Christians. The entire New Testament was composed solely in Greek.[2] As the Apostles spread the message of Christ throughout the Roman Empire, they relied on the Septuagint version of the Old Testament since their Gentile audience would not have been able to understand the Hebrew texts. Greek had become the common language of every metropolitan city from Egypt to Rome. The Apostles preached from the Septuagint, and it was the Septuagint that the Apostles employed when they wrote the New Testament. Concerning all the quotations of the Old Testament found in the New Testament—one hundred quotations correspond to the Septuagint text, while only six correspond with the received Masoretic Hebrew text. Thus, the New Testament gives evidence that the Apostles rarely employed the Hebrew texts.

When Pope Saint Damasus (d. A.D. 383) commissioned Saint Jerome to produce a new Latin translation of the Sacred Scriptures, Saint Jerome checked the Greek Septuagint against the Hebrew version available to him. Saint Jerome believed that the Hebrew text was superior to the Greek Septuagint version of the Old Testament. As a result of his reversion to the Hebrew text, Saint Jerome received great criticism, since the Septuagint version seemed to be the official version ratified by the Apostles. Nevertheless, Saint Jerome's timeless Vulgate is based on the Hebrew text and not the Greek text of the Septuagint. Regardless of Saint Jerome's decision, the Septuagint Greek translation of the Hebrew Bible is the most lasting legacy of the Greek influence over Judaism—an influence retained to this day in the pages of the New Testament.

The Maccabees and the Jews in Palestine

The Septuagint proved to be a positive development under the Third Kingdom of Greece, but that is not what stands out most clearly in the history of Jewish-Greek relations. Jerusalem remained unmolested by the Greeks until trouble came in 175 B.C. with the infamous Greco-Syrian king Antiochus IV Epiphanes of Seleucid dynasty. The title *Epiphanes* refers to Antiochus' claim to be "God-manifested." It is not surprising that the Jews were going to run into conflict with their new "God-manifested" king. The Jews instead referred to their king as Antiochus IV *Epimanes*–Antiochus IV *the Crazy*. Little did he know, Antiochus IV Epiphanes was about to enter a hornets' nest. Hellenization could only go so far with the Jews living in Palestine.

During this time, what was once the Greek Empire began to disintegrate as it felt pressure from the emerging Italian city-state of Rome. Antiochus IV himself had been held as a political hostage in Rome following the peace of Apamea in 188 B.C. The Romans bartered Antiochus IV for the son and rightful heir to the Seleucid throne—Seleucus IV (later Demetrius I Soter). Now that Antiochus IV was free and the rightful heir was imprisoned in Rome, Antiochus proclaimed himself vice-regent of the infant son of Seleucus. One year later he had the child murdered, and lo and behold, Antiochus IV was the sole ruler of the Seleucid kingdom.

In 168 B.C., the navy of Antiochus IV conquered Cyprus and Egypt with the exception of the great port city of Alexandria. Near Alexandria Antiochus IV was met by the Roman envoy Gaius Popillius Laenas. Popillius commanded Antiochus IV to withdraw immediately from both Egypt and Cyprus. Antiochus IV began to stall for time and explained that he would have to consult with his council. Immediately Popillius had a circle drawn around Antiochus IV and said, "Think about it here!" Popillius implied that if he did not withdraw from both Egypt and Cyprus, Rome would declare war against Antiochus IV. Antiochus reluctantly complied with the Roman mandate and withdrew.

As Antiochus IV left Egypt and passed through the Holy Land, he let out his fury against Jerusalem. On the fifteenth day of the Jewish month of Chislev, or December 6, in 167 B.C. (1 Macc. 1:54), Antiochus IV ordered an image of Zeus to be erected in the temple of Jerusalem, burnt incense to the Greek gods, publicly burned copies of the Hebrew Scriptures, and issued decrees in Judea forbidding Jewish religious practice in favor of Greek paganism. Needless to say, this didn't go over well.

Ten days later, Antiochus IV did the unthinkable. It is common knowledge that pigs were unclean to Jews. Antiochus IV either didn't consult his public relations team or he was out to infuriate the Jews. History indicates the latter, because on the twenty-fifth day of the month of Chislev, or December 16 (1 Macc. 1:59), Antiochus ordered that a pig be sacrificed on the Altar of the Lord in the Temple complex of Jerusalem. This act defiled not only the altar, but also the Temple, which had now been declared as a Temple of Zeus and not of the Lord of Israel.

When the pig had been cooked upon the altar, Jewish men were compelled to eat the unclean swine's flesh. They refused even to the point of having their tongues cut out by the soldiers of Antiochus IV. The soldiers eventually scalped these Jewish men, cut off their hands and feet, and then burned their tongues and appendages on the altar of the Lord.

Antiochus IV forbade the keeping of the Sabbath, and the Greek customs of idolatry and nude gymnasiums were encouraged. If it became known that a child had been circumcised in accordance with the Law of Moses, the family was murdered and the circumcised child was hung from the neck of his dead mother. All over Judea, Jews were enjoined to eat swine's flesh in violation of the Jewish kosher laws of ceremonial purity. Things were reaching a boiling point. The Jewish people were enraged.

Yet when all seemed lost, God elevated a military genius around which the faithful Jews would rally. When the Greek forces came to Modiin in order to assimilate the population to Hellenistic customs, a Jewish priest named Mattathias the Hasmonean became that hero. Mattathias slew a conforming Hellenistic Jew who dared to betray the commandments of Moses by worshiping an idol. This action sparked a Jewish revolt, and Mattathias and his five sons John, Simon, Eleazar,

Jonathan, and Judah fled to the desserts of Judea in order to lead an attack against the Greco-Syrian occupation of Antiochus IV *the Crazy*.

Mattathias died in battle one year later in 166 B.C., and his son Judas Maccabaeus ("Judah the Hammer") led the zealous army of Jewish warriors against the Greco-Syrian occupiers. This army was known by their leader's title—the Maccabees. Antiochus IV sent to Judea an army of 40,000 infantry and 7,000 cavalry. Against all odds, the backwoods army of Judas Maccabaeus defeated the world's greatest superpower in a series of successful battles. The Greco-Syrian armies were distressed by the Maccabees unconventional guerilla tactics, a practice similar to that used by the American revolutionists against the English in the eighteenth century.

The victory of Judas Maccabaeus coincided with the third anniversary of the blasphemous pig sacrifice on Antiochus IV on Chislev 25, 167 B.C. So on Chislev 25, 164 B.C., Judas Maccabaeus triumphantly marched into Jerusalem and ritually cleansed the Temple. The altar on which the pig had been slaughtered was torn apart and a new altar was built and dedicated. The Jews of Jerusalem celebrated an eight-day festival to rededicate their Temple to the God of Israel. Judas Maccabaeus and all the assembly of Israel decreed that this event should be commemorated every year "with joy and gladness for eight days." This was the birth of the eight-day festival of *Hanukkah*, meaning "Dedication," because it marks the rededication of the Temple by the Maccabees after it had been desecrated by the idolatry and unclean sacrifice of Antiochus IV. The full account of these events, including the lurid details about the tyrannous acts of Antiochus IV can be read in the biblical accounts of 1 and 2 Maccabees.

According to tradition, Judas Maccabaeus could only obtain enough consecrated olive oil to fuel the

Temple's menorah for one day. Miraculously, the holy oil burned for the length of eight days—just in time for the priests to press olives and properly consecrate a new batch of holy oil. However, the original reason for the eight days of Hanukkah is that the festival is intended to resemble the eight-day feast of Tabernacles, which was the occasion on which King Solomon dedicated the original Temple in Jerusalem. If eight days of dedication were good enough for Solomon the Wise, then eight days of dedication were good enough for Judas Maccabaeus.

For our interests, Judas Maccabaeus is the first link between Jerusalem and Rome.

> Now Judas heard of the fame of the Romans, that they were very strong and were well-disposed toward all who made an alliance with them, that they pledged friendship to those who came to them, and that they were very strong. (1 Macc 8:1-2)

The newfound independence of Jerusalem was fragile, and the Jews desperately needed an ally to defend them from the Syrian threat to their north. Judas therefore sent ambassadors to Rome to establish an alliance (1 Macc 8). The Jews were impressed with the senatorial principles of the Roman Republic and felt somewhat assured that an alliance with the Roman Republic would preserve them from the tyranny they had experienced under Antiochus IV:

> Yet for all this not one of [the Romans] has put on a crown or worn purple as a mark of pride, but they have built for themselves a senate chamber, and every day three hundred and twenty senators constantly deliberate concerning the people, to govern

them well. They trust one man each year to
rule over them and to control all their land;
they all heed the one man, and there is no
envy or jealousy among them (1 Macc 8:14-
16).

The Roman senate was constantly concerned with
Syrian trade and desperately needed a Middle Eastern
ally. Judea provided the perfect buffer between Syria
and Egypt. In an era of Greek dominance, Jerusalem
and Rome established a treaty and became allies.
According to the first book of Maccabees, the Romans
received the Jewish ambassadors of Judas Maccabeus
and responded with a reply engraved on bronze tablets:

Good success be to the Romans, and to the people
of the Jews by sea, and by land, for ever: and far be
the sword and enemy from them. But if there come
first any war upon the Romans, or any of their
confederates, in all their dominions: The nation of
the Jews shall help them according as the time shall
direct, with all their heart: Neither shall they give
them, whilst they are fighting, or furnish them with
wheat, or arms, or money, or ships, as it hath
seemed good to the Romans: and they shall obey
their orders, without taking any thing of them.

In like manner also if war shall come first upon the
nation of the Jews, the Romans shall help them with
all their heart, according as the time shall permit
them: And there shall not be given to them that
come to their aid, either wheat, or arms, or money,
or ships, as it hath seemed good to the Romans: and
they shall observe their orders without deceit.

According to these articles did the Romans
covenant with the people of the Jews. And, if after

this, one party or the other shall have a mind to add to these articles, or take away any thing, they may do it at their pleasure: and whatsoever they shall add, or take away, shall be ratified (1 Macc 8:23-30).

And so the Jews and the Romans became allies. Rome gambled with Jerusalem and put down the Seleucid threat to the East. Jerusalem made a wager with Rome and gained their independence—that is until Rome was ready to take it away.

Jewish Independence or Roman Dependence?

The nephew of Judas Maccabaeus became the Jewish High Priest in 134 B.C. His name was John Hyrcanus. During this time the High Priest of Jerusalem became the *de facto* ruler of Judea. Many Jews did not accept him as king because he was not of the Messianic line of King David. For this reason he bore the title *Nasi* ("Prince"). Moreover, many Jews did not even accept him as a true High Priest because he was not of the line of Aaron. Nevertheless, John Hyrcanus functioned as both priest and king of the Jews.

John Hyrcanus was, shall we say, controversial. He had the Samaritan temple on Mt. Gerizim demolished, an act that deepened the centuries-old rivalry between the Jews and the Samaritans. It also seems that the divide between Pharisees and Sadducees arose during his reign. He also waged war against the neighboring Idumeans—the descendants of the biblical Edomites in Judea—and forced them at sword point to convert to Judaism. The priestly class of the Sadducee party seems to have developed from supporters of John Hyrcanus, while the Pharisees maintained doubts about the legitimacy of John's claim to the High Priesthood.

Sadducees were what you might call Temple Jews or Jewish minimalists. Their name derives from *Zadok*, the name of the High Priest from the days of King David and King Solomon. The religion of the Sadducees was strictly concerned with the Temple, priests, vestments, sacrifices, and feast days prescribed by Moses. They held that anything not found in the five books of Moses (Genesis, Exodus, Leviticus, Numbers, and Deuteronomy) was not binding upon Jews. They did not believe in angels, life after death, the resurrection of the body, and they did not likely have any expectation of a coming Messiah.

On the other hand, there were the Pharisees. Their name derives from the Hebrew word *Parushim*, meaning "the separated ones." Unlike the Sadducees, the Pharisees subscribed to not only the books of Moses, but to the entire Hebrew Old Testament. Pharisees were concerned about keeping themselves pure before God. This was hard work, and it required many rules. The Pharisees believed that individual Jews were called to imitate the ceremonial purity of the priests in Jerusalem. They collected a huge body of traditions concerning what was "clean" and "unclean." These new customs surpassed the regulations of Moses.

The Pharisees' desire to be "clean" meant that they refused to associate with Gentiles. The Pharisees might be best understood as "Jewish Puritans." They also began to wear clothing and other paraphernalia that denoted them as observant Jews. These external signs of distinction became more and more pronounced as time passed. They wore phylacteries on their foreheads that contained passages of Scripture and wore conspicuous tassels that revealed that they were truly observant Jews. Pharisees were greatly concerned with keeping the Sabbath. They were scrupulous about what constituted "work on the Sabbath."

With the rise of the Sadducee party around John Hyrcanus, the spiritual integrity of the kingdom of Judea began to decline. His son Aristobulus I was reckless.

Unlike his father, who bore only the title of High Priest and Prince, Aristobulus assumed the title of King of Judea. According to the dying wishes of John Hyrcanus, the government of the country after his death was to be placed in the hands of his wife, and his son Aristobulus was to receive only the High Priesthood. However, Aristobulus was not content with this arrangement. He threw his mother into prison where she starved to death. He persecuted the Pharisee party, and after a one-year rule he died of a painful illness in 103 B.C.

Alexander Jannaeus succeeded his brother Aristobulus. The pro-Hellenist Sadducee party rallied around Alexander, and he waged a civil war against the Pharisee party. He aligned himself with the Essenes, the monastic movement responsible for the Dead Sea Scrolls. He showed considerable competence as a military leader, repelling invaders and expanding the country's borders to the west and south. He made an alliance with Cleopatra and drove Ptolemy out of Galilee. By the end of his rule, the borders of his kingdom would exceed that of King David and extend to Gaza and far into Jordan. Upon his death, he was succeeded as regent by his wife Salome Alexandra, known better as Shelomtzion, and was succeeded as High Priest by his son John Hyrcanus II.

John Hyrcanus II served as the Jewish High Priest from about 79 to 40 B.C. His reigning mother named him as her successor to the throne. He had sat on the throne for only three months when his younger brother, Aristobulus II, rebelled against him. John Hyrcanus II rallied the Sadducee party and met his brother in battle near Jericho. Aristobulus II prevailed and John Hyrcanus II surrendered to his little brother by renouncing the High Priesthood.

The plot thickens. In 64 B.C. the Roman general Pompey came to Syria and annexed the kingdom as a Roman province. He realized that the feuding brothers of Judea had considerably weakened the Jews and that the nation was out of control. Now was the time to bring Judea under the rule of Rome. When Pompey seized Jerusalem and overtook it in 63 B.C., he was amazed that the Jews did not have any image or likeness of their God. Out of curiosity he entered into the Holy of Holies to see if the Jews possessed any kind of image in their Temple. Pompey found nothing – not even the Ark of the Covenant. He was only the second person ever to violate the Holy of Holies. This action symbolized the end of the Jewish independence. Once again the Jewish people found themselves under the rule of the idolatrous Gentiles. "King" Aristobulus II and "King" John Hyrcanus II had sacrificed the independence of Judea by their envy and greed. Judea was no longer an independent ally of Rome – it now belonged to Rome.

NOTES

[2] The Gospel of Saint Matthew was originally written in Aramaic, but its canonical form was received by the Church in Greek.

3. THE BIRTH OF CHRIST UNDER CAESAR

If He had chosen the great city of Rome, the change in the world would be ascribed to the influence of her citizens. If He had been the son of the Emperor, His benefits would have been attributed to the latter's power. But that we might acknowledge the work of God in the transformation of the whole earth, He chose a poor mother and a birthplace poorer still.

- Council of Ephesus, A.D. 431

IN 49 B.C. JULIUS CAESAR assumed the throne as Dictator of the Roman Empire. Two years later Caesar reappointed John Hyrcanus II as the titular High Priest and appointed Antipater of the Idumeans as the first Roman Procurator (i.e. King) of Judea. The great irony was that John Hyrcanus *the First* had forced the Idumeans to convert to Judaism and now an Idumean had become the King of Judea over John Hyrcanus *the Second.*

Julius Caesar was stabbed to death in 44 B.C. One year later, Antipater the King of Judea was poisoned. The son of Antipater fled into exile, unsure of where fate would place him. His name was Herod.

Herod sought protection from Mark Antony, the famous lover of Cleopatra. Mark Antony proved to be a useful friend to Herod. In 40 B.C. Mark Antony went before the Roman Senate in order to have Herod named *King of the Jews*:

> ...telling them that it was for their advantage in the Parthian war that Herod should be king; so they all gave their votes for it. And when the senate was separated, Antony and Caesar [Augustus] went out, with Herod between them. Meanwhile the consul and the rest of the magistrates went before them, in order to offer sacrifices, and to lay the decree in the Capitol. Antony also made a feast for Herod on the first day of his reign.[3]

Herod returned to Jerusalem with a Roman army of 60,000 soldiers in order to persuade the Jews that he was in fact the new "King of the Jews." Judea reluctantly accepted their new king. Incidentally, this episode in Jewish history initiated an important debate in first-century Judaism: Who is *truly* the King of the Jews?

Herod the Great was a villain. He had a total of ten wives. He murdered his favorite wife on account of jealousy and killed three of his own sons. Herod betrayed his patron Mark Antony, siding with Octavian when he perceived that Octavian held the upper hand over Mark Antony.

Even though King Herod was an Idumean, he claimed that he was a Jew. Technically, he was circumcised and confessed faith in the God of Israel, but he was not an ethnic Israelite. Herod spread a story that he was in fact an ethnic Jew, but almost everyone knew that this was not the case. His true allegiance fell to Rome, and Rome expected only two things from Herod the Great: keep the peace and collect taxes. Herod kept the peace by rebuilding the temple complex on a scale that rivaled even King Solomon's Temple.

Observant Jews may have despised Herod, but they did appreciate the Temple. Pilgrims from all over the world came to Jerusalem in order to behold the great Temple of the Jews. The influx of pilgrims boosted the economy, which in return allowed more taxes to be sent to Rome.

Peace and pilgrimages brought economic health to Judea. Of course, there were problems. The compromised Sadducees controlled the Temple and the sacrifices. A pseudo-Jew ruled the nation. Technically, Jerusalem belonged to Rome. But life was good. Herod became Herod the Great. He was invincible. He was backed by the world's greatest superpower, the Roman Empire. The Fourth Beast of Daniel was about to open its mouth against the Messiah.

Rome and the Fullness of Time

The Apostle Paul wrote, "But when the time had fully come, God sent forth his Son, born of woman, born under the law, to redeem those who were under the law, so that we might receive adoption as sons" (Gal 4:4-5). For Paul and the early Christians, Christ was born in "the fullness of time." In other words, God chose this specific era to bring about His redemption through Christ.

As described in Chapter 1, the book of Daniel depicts the advent of the Son of Man occurring in the era of the Fourth Kingdom, that is, the Roman Empire. At last, the time had come. The Roman Empire was secure. Octavian Caesar, the adopted son of Julius Caesar, had defeated both Pompey and Mark Antony at the Battle of Actium in 31 B.C. Octavian Caesar emerged as the sole ruler of the Roman Empire. Octavian Caesar was given the new title Caesar Augustus, and the *Pax Romana* settled upon the entire known world. Roman roads extended out from every major city. Rome ruled over what is today Spain, Britain, Western Europe, Greece, Turkey, Syria, Palestine, the entire coast along North Africa from Egypt to the Strait of Gibraltar, and every island to be named within the Mediterranean Sea.

By this time, Jews could be found in every major city in the Roman Empire. It is estimated that about seven percent of the population of the empire was Jewish. These Jews carried their beliefs and Scriptures throughout the world. Jewish synagogues had been founded all over the Roman Empire. In the synagogues, Jews came together on the Sabbath to pray, read the Scriptures, and listen to the rabbis expound the sacred texts. The synagogues of the empire provided the original outposts of evangelism for the Apostles as they went out into the world to proclaim the Gospel of Jesus Christ. Greek was still the *lingua franca* of the empire and the Septuagint provided the Jewish Scriptures in a language accessible to non-Jews. Everything was set in place so that God could spread message of the Messiah to the Gentiles.

It seems that the Jews were not the only ones waiting for a Savior. There is a strong tradition that even pagan seers began to prophesy of the coming Christ who would be a heavenly child and king of the world. The prophetic voice of the classical world belonged to sibyls. The word *sibyl* comes from the Greek word *sibylla*, which means "prophetess." The sibyls were women who uttered prophetic oracles at shrines or temples throughout the classical world.

Visitors to the Vatican are sometimes amazed to learn that pagan sibyls are included along with the Israelite prophets on the ceiling of the Sistine Chapel. Michelangelo included five sibyls on the ceiling of the Sistine Chapel since each prophesied of the coming of Christ:

Erythræan Sibyl
Persian Sibyl
Libyan Sibyl
Cumæan Sibyl
Delphic Sibyl

These prophecies of the Sibyls were well known in the ancient world. For example, Virgil quotes the Cumæan Sibyl in his fourth Eclogue:

Now the last age of Cumæan Verses is come,
Afresh the great cycle of ages begins,
Returns the Virgin, Saturnian Kingdoms return,
The heavenly Offspring descends from on high.[4]

This was written before the birth of Christ, and yet Virgil acknowledges the Cumæan sibyls prophecy that a Virgin would bring forth a heavenly child from on high. Compare Virgil's words to those of Saint Gabriel to the Blessed Virgin Mary: "The Holy Spirit will come upon you, and the power of the Most High will overshadow you; therefore the child to be born will be called holy, the Son of God" (Lk 1:35).

Cicero, the Roman orator and philosopher wrote "It has been announced in ancient prophecies that a king is to appear, to whom men must do homage in order to be saved."[5] The Roman historian Suetonius wrote that "throughout the East an old and constant opinion was frequently expressed to the effect men starting from Judea were destine at that time to acquire the world-wide supremacy."[6] The Roman historian Tacitus concurs:

Men were convinced that it was written in
the ancient books of the priests that at that
very time the East should grow strong and

men starting from Judea should acquire the supremacy.[7]

We read in the Gospel of Saint Matthew that Jesus Christ was born under the reign of Caesar Augustus. The reader should feel the political tension between the success of Caesar and birth of a mysterious baby acclaimed as the king of heaven *and earth*. The supernatural Kingdom of God has crashed into the Fourth Kingdom of this world as described in the second chapter of Daniel. Christ would later answer a nervous Pilate with the striking statement: "My kingdom is not of this world" (Jn 18:36).

The Angel Gabriel came to a young teenage maiden named Mary who lived under Roman rule. The message is amazing. According to the visions of Saint Elizabeth of Hungary, the Blessed Virgin Mary was praying for the coming of the Messiah at the very moment the Angel Gabriel arrived. Gabriel announced:

> "Hail, full of grace, the Lord is with you!"

> But she was greatly troubled at the saying, and considered in her mind what sort of greeting this might be (Lk 1:29).

Regarding this angelic salutation of Gabriel, the Blessed Virgin Mary herself related the following information to Saint Mechtilde of Hackeborn (died in 1298):

> My daughter, I want you to know that no one can please me more by saying the salutation which the Most Adorable Trinity sent to me and by which He raised me to the dignity of Mother of God. By the word "Ave," which is the name Eve, I learned that in His infinite power God has preserved me

from all sin and its attendant misery which
the first woman had been subject to.[8]

Moderns would likely dismiss Saint Mechtilde's account
as pious fiction for the simple fact that the Blessed
Virgin Mary would not have likely received the angelic
salutation in Latin with the Latin greeting *Ave*. Rather,
the Greek of Saint Luke's Gospel reads *Chaire*, not the
Latin *Ave*.

There is, however, something to Saint Mechtilde's
revelation. The Catholic commentator Cornelius a
Lapide makes an excellent observation. Saint Gabriel
would have addressed Mary in Hebrew, and likely would
have begun his annunciation with the Hebrew greeting
"cha-ve" meaning "Live," as in "Long live the king" or
"Viva Papa" or "Viva Cristo Rey." Now then, according
to Genesis 3:20, the Hebrew name of Eve is "cha-va"
meaning "living" because, as the Holy Spirit explains,
Eve is the "Mother of the Living."

This shows that there is indeed a mystical meaning
in the original Hebrew greeting of Gabriel to Mary, and
that the Virgin's explanation to Saint Mechtilde is
linguistically accurate within the limits of Hebraic
vocabulary. Moreover, this linguistic commonality
further establishes Mary as the New Eve. It also reveals
that the Latin Vulgate version captures the original
Semitic meaning through an Indo-European root.

Returning to the angelic greeting, Saint Gabriel
continued by saying:

> "Do not be afraid, Mary, for you have found
> favor with God. And behold, you will
> conceive in your womb and bear a son, and
> you shall call his name Jesus. He will be
> great, and will be called the Son of the Most
> High; and the Lord God will give to him the
> throne of his father David, and he will reign

over the house of Jacob for ever; and of his kingdom there will be no end."

And Mary said to the angel, "How shall this be, since I have no husband?"

And the angel said to her, "The Holy Spirit will come upon you, and the power of the Most High will overshadow you; therefore the child to be born will be called holy, the Son of God. And behold, your kinswoman Elizabeth in her old age has also conceived a son; and this is the sixth month with her who was called barren. For with God nothing will be impossible."

And Mary said, "Behold, I am the handmaid of the Lord; let it be to me according to your word." And the angel departed from her (Lk 1:28-38).

Mary, then, was the predestined mother of the long-expected Messiah. But there is something else that is startling—the identity of the messenger. It is Gabriel, whose name means *Mighty Man of God*. Gabriel's role in the Annunciation is significant because Gabriel only appears in one other book of the Bible, the Book of Daniel. It would seem that Gabriel's name meaning *Mighty Man of God* refers to his role in proclaiming the Incarnation of God the Son—the true Mighty Man of God.

It is the Angel Gabriel who explains to Daniel the time of the Messiah's birth. Gabriel explains that the Messiah will appear publicly after "sixty-nine weeks" (Dan 9:20, 25). Sixty-nine weeks is another way of saying sixty-nine sevens (69 x 7 = 483) or 483 years. The 483-year countdown begins, according to Gabriel, "from the going forth of the word to restore and build Jerusalem to the coming of an anointed one" (Dan 9:25).

The "going forth of the word to restore and build Jerusalem" occurred when King Artaxerxes issued the proclamation to restore and rebuild Jerusalem in 453 B.C. (Dan 9:25). If we follow the calculation given by the Archangel Gabriel to Daniel and measure out 483 years from the date of 453 B.C., we arrive at the date of A.D. 30, the time of Christ's baptism and the beginning of His public ministry. It is Gabriel who tells Daniel the exact date of the Messiah's appearance in A.D. 30. It is not surprising then that God sent the same angel to announce to Mary that the time had come for the Messiah to be born so that He would be ready to begin His ministry by A.D. 30.

Now Saint Gabriel explained that one more week of *seven years* shall follow after A.D. 30. During this time, "the Messiah shall be cut off, but not for himself" (Dan 9:26). In other words, the Messiah shall die not for Himself, but for others. Saint Gabriel explains to Daniel that this will happen at after "half the week" (Dan 9:27) or three and a half years after A.D. 30. Three and a half years after A.D. 30 brings us to A.D. 33—the year of Christ's death on the cross. Gabriel foretells the death of the Messiah down to the exact year. The final three and a half years end in A.D. 36, the time marking the vision of Saint Peter in the ninth chapter of Acts which initiated the inclusion of the Gentiles into the Catholic Church. This time also marks the conversion of Saint Paul and his apostolic mission to the Gentiles.

When Caesar Augustus called for a census of the Roman Empire, he had ruled the Empire for more than a quarter of a century. God chose this Roman Emperor to fulfill an obscure Jewish prophecy—that the Messiah should be born in Bethlehem:

> But you, O Bethlehem Ephrathah,
> who are little to be among the clans of Judah,
> from you shall come forth for me
> one who is to be ruler in Israel,
> whose origin is from of old,
> from ancient days (Mic 5:2).

Until this time, Joseph and Mary had lived in Nazareth, and it appeared that the miraculous baby of Mary would be born there. Caesar intervened, and Joseph found himself packing up his pregnant wife for the ninety-mile journey from Nazareth to Bethlehem. We are only told that Joseph went to Bethlehem, "because he was of the house and lineage of David" (Luke 2:4). Joseph likely felt the need to go to Bethlehem in order to ensure that he would not forfeit land that was his by inheritance. In America, we are required to vote in the state of our residence. Failure to prove residence results in giving up the right to vote in that state. We can only conjecture why Joseph felt compelled to travel to Bethlehem. As a carpenter, Joseph was able to work anywhere. However, for official purposes, he likely wanted to be reckoned with his historic place of origin.

It would have taken about four or five days to travel the distance between Nazareth and Bethlehem. Bethlehem was not only the prophetic birthplace of the future Messiah, but also it had been the birthplace of King David and the site of his anointing as the King of Israel. The Blessed Virgin Mary knew these details, and she would have recalled the words of the Angel Gabriel:

> He will be great, and will be called the Son
> of the Most High; and the Lord God will
> give to him the throne of *his father David*, and
> *he will reign over the house of Jacob for ever*, and of
> *his kingdom there will be no end*" (Lk 1:32-33).

As the Blessed Virgin Mary pondered all these things in her heart, she likely began to realize that the prophetic voices of the Old Covenant were falling into harmony. It was indeed the fullness of time.

Apparition of Mary to Caesar

The Roman reign of Caesar Augustus was an era of peace, prosperity, and felicity. Augustus took an imperial census during this era of peace, at which time he closed the temple of Janus for the third time, in the fortieth year of his reign. The Prince of Peace would be born into this historical parenthesis of peace. According to Saint Bede the Venerable, "A lover of peace, He would be born in a time of the most profound quiet. And there could be no plainer indication of peace than that a census should be taken of the whole world, whose master Augustus was, having reigned at the time of Christ's nativity for some twelve years in the greatest peace, war being lulled to sleep throughout all the world."[9]

Tradition holds that Caesar Augustus learned from the oracle of the Tiburtine Sybil that a Hebrew child would silence all the oracles of the Roman gods. Tradition also records that the Blessed Virgin Mary, holding the Christ Child in her arms, appeared to Caesar Augustus on the Capitol Hill. Augustus recognized that this vision corresponded to the oracle concerning the Hebrew child. In response to this apparition of Mary and Jesus, Augustus built an altar in the Capitol in honor of this child with the title *Ara Primogeniti Dei,* meaning "Altar of the Firstborn of God." Over three hundred years later, the Christian emperor Constantine the Great built a church at this location of the apparition and altar, which is called *Basilica Sanctae Mariae de Ara Coeli,* meaning "Basilica of Saint Mary of the Altar of Heaven."[10] If one visits the church today, he will observe murals of Caesar Augustus and of the Tiburtine Sibyl painted on either side of the arch above the high altar. These images recall the oracle, which prophesied the advent of the Hebrew "Firstborn of God." In the fifteenth century, this church became famous for a statue of the Christ Child carved from olive wood taken from the Garden of Gethsemane outside Jerusalem. The church's connection to the birth of Christ made it a fitting place for devotion to the infancy of the Savior.

Meanwhile in the Jewish district of Rome, on the day of Christ's nativity, a fountain of oil flowed out from the earth in the tavern of a certain man in what is today called *Trastevere*—the region south of the Vatican and to the west of the Tiber River. This fountain of oil revealed to the Jews of Rome that the Messiah had at last been born, since Messiah or Christ means "anointed with oil." To this very day, the Church of Saint Maria in Trastevere marks the location. The Emperor Septimius Severus, who reigned from A.D. 193 to 211, granted the location to the Christians. In A.D. 220, Pope Saint Callixtus I established the site as a church, and his relics still remain under the church's high altar. The church has been rebuilt several times and can still be visited to this very day.

The Birth Year of Christ

As you know, B.C. refers to "before Christ" and it is therefore confusing to hear scholars say that Christ was born in 4 B.C. This would mean that Christ was born four years *before Christ*. However, recent and more precise chronological studies have validated the traditional date of Christ's birth at December 25 in 1 B.C.[11]

As way of background, the dating of B.C. (before Christ) and A.D. (*anno Domini* or year of the Lord) derives from the calculations of the Dionysius Exiguus. Exiguus means *little*, so he is often called Dionysius the Little. Dionysius was a Scythian monk living in Rome. He died in about A.D. 544. Incidentally, when you write dates, B.C. goes after the number and A.D. goes in front of it. For example:

754 B.C.

or

A.D. 1492

In Rome, Dionysius worked with the best Roman records and Church documents to compute the birth of Christ. This new computation divided time before and after Christ. Dionysius did not include a year zero. December 31 in 1 B.C. would have passed to January 1 in A.D. 1.

Now Dionysius identified Gabriel's annunciation to the Virgin and the incarnation of Christ in the womb of the Blessed Virgin Mary on March 25 in the year 1 B.C. He recognized the birthday of Christ as being December 25 in the year 1 B.C. The circumcision of Christ, eight days after His birth, was on January 1 of A.D. 1. His crucifixion was in the year A.D. 33.

The Venerable Bede took up the dating scheme of Dionysius the Little in his *Ecclesiastical History of the English People*, and the rest is history. We still use his dating system to this day—B.C. and A.D.

Doubts over the birth year of Christ arose in the 1600s. Scholars became aware of the chronology provided by the Jewish historian Josephus. Josephus places the death of King Herod the Great in what Dionysius called 4 B.C. Since Herod tried to kill the infant Christ, then it would necessarily be the case that Christ would be born before the death of Herod. If

Herod died in 4 B.C., then Christ would need to be born before 4 B.C. And so, ever since the seventeenth century, people have been claiming that Dionysius got it wrong and that Christ was born four years *before Christ.*

What do we make of all this? Well, either Josephus is correct or Dionysius is correct. Both cannot be right. Until recently most scholars agreed with Josephus because: A) Josephus lived in the century of Christ, B) Josephus was Jewish, and C) Josephus was a professional historian. Dionysius was just a monk living in Rome over five hundred years later.

However, there is now good reason for believing that Josephus got it wrong. Further studies of Josephus reveal that he was most certainly not consistent or accurate in dating several key events in Jewish and Roman history. In fact, Josephus contradicts verified history, the Bible, and even his own chronology about one hundred times. His dates are not very accurate. The French archaeologist, jurist, and historian Theodore Reinarch was one of the first to document the many factual and chronological errors of Josephus. Reinarch's translation of Josephus is steadily interrupted by comments such as "this is a mistake" or "in another book his figures are different."[12]

The following is an example of the poor chronology of Josephus. Josephus records in his *Jewish War* that Hyrcanus reigned for thirty-three years. Yet in his *Antiquities of the Jews,* that Hyrcanus reigned thirty-two years.[13] Yet in another place in his *Antiquities,* Josephus says that Hyrcanus reigned only thirty years. That's three contradictory claims—two in the same book!

In his *Jewish War,* Josephus records that Aristobulus set the diadem on his head 471 years after the exile. Yet in his *Antiquities,* he says it was 481 years, a ten-year difference. By the way, modern historians now know that it was 490 years. Josephus is wrong on all accounts.

More examples could be supplied. The fact is that Josephus was sloppy with dates, especially when they regarded monarchs. So let us take a look at the dates he gives for King Herod. We discover that Josephus actually gave two contradictory dates for the death of Herod—4 B.C. and A.D. 7 or 8.

Josephus writes that Herod captured Jerusalem and began to rule in what Dionysius would call 37 B.C., and that Herod lived for 34 years after this. If you do the math, this means that Herod died in 4 or 3 B.C. Scholars site this as the authoritative proof that Jesus was born before 4-3 B.C.

However, Josephus records a different dating for the death of Herod elsewhere. In his *Antiquities*, Josephus writes that Herod was fifteen years old in what we would call 47 B.C. when Caesar appointed Hyrcanus as ethnarch.[14] But, twice elsewhere Josephus states that Herod was seventy years old when he died. So if Herod was 15 in 47 B.C., that means he died at age 70 in either A.D. 7 or A.D. 8.

We have a serious discrepancy in the dates of Josephus—a window of more than ten years. Moreover, who really knows if either number is accurate given his mistakes on other historical dates?

Why is this important? It reveals that we should not allow Josephus to have the last word on the chronology of Christ. Josephus' dating of Herod's death to 4 B.C. is truly only one version of his calculations. Why not use his date of A.D. 7 or 8? It is rather arbitrary for modern historians to endorse the date of 4 B.C.

The best way to date Herod's death is by focusing on the testimony that Herod died a few months after a well-observed lunar eclipse. With modern astronomical models, we know that such a lunar eclipse occurred at Jerusalem before sunset on December 29 in 1 B.C. This would mean that Herod died sometime after A.D. 1. This lines up perfectly with the chronology of Dionysius

the Little. Now what about the date? Was Christ truly
born on December 25 in 1 B.C.?

Was Christ Born on December 25?

The Catholic Church, from at least the second
century, has claimed that Christ was born on December
25. However, it is commonly alleged that our Lord Jesus
Christ was not born on December 25. For the sake of
simplicity, let us set out the usual objections to the date
of December 25 and counter each of them.

Objection 1: December 25 was chosen in order to
replace the pagan Roman festival of
Saturnalia. Saturnalia was a popular winter festival and
so the Catholic Church prudently substituted Christmas
in its place.

Reply to Objection 1: Saturnalia commemorated the
winter solstice. Yet the winter solstice falls on
December 22. It is true that Saturnalia celebrations
began as early as December 17 and extended till
December 23. Still, the dates don't match up.

Objection 2: December 25 was chosen to replace the
pagan Roman holiday *Natalis Solis Invicti* which means
"Birthday of the Unconquered Sun."

Reply to Objection 2: Let us examine first the cult of
the Unconquered Sun. The Emperor Aurelian
introduced the cult of the *Sol Invictus* or *Unconquered Sun*
to Rome in A.D. 274. Aurelian found political traction
with this cult, because his own name *Aurelian* derives
from the Latin word *aurora* denoting "sunrise." Coins
reveal that Emperor Aurelian called himself the *Pontifex
Solis* or *Pontiff of the Sun*. Thus, Aurelian simply

accommodated a generic solar cult and identified his name with it at the end of the third century.

Most importantly, there is no historical record for a celebration *Natalis Sol Invictus* on December 25 prior to A.D. 354. Within an illuminated manuscript for the year A.D. 354, there is an entry for December 25 reading "N INVICTI CM XXX." Here N means "nativity." INVICTI means "of the Unconquered." CM signifies "circenses missus" or "games ordered." The Roman numeral XXX equals thirty. Thus, the inscription means that thirty games were ordered for the nativity of the Unconquered for December 25th. Note that the word "sun" is not present. Moreover, the very same codex also lists "natus Christus in Betleem Iudeae" for the day of December 25. The phrase is translated as "birth of Christ in Bethlehem of Judea."[15]

The date of December 25th only became the "Birthday of the Unconquered Sun" under the Emperor Julian the Apostate. Julian the Apostate had been a Christian but who had apostatized and returned to Roman paganism. History reveals that it was the hateful former Christian Emperor that erected a pagan holiday on December 25. Think about that for a moment. What was he trying to replace?

These historical facts reveal that the Unconquered Sun was not likely a popular deity in the Roman Empire. The Roman people did not need to be weaned off of a so-called ancient holiday. Moreover, the tradition of a December 25th celebration does not find a place on the Roman calendar *until after the Christianization of Rome*. The "Birthday of the Unconquered Sun" holiday was scarcely traditional and hardly popular. Saturnalia (mentioned above) was much more popular, traditional, and fun. It seems, rather, that Julian the Apostate had attempted to introduce a pagan holiday in order to replace the Christian one!

Objection 3: Christ could not have been born in December since Saint Luke describes shepherds herding in the neighboring fields of Bethlehem. Shepherds do not herd during the winter. Thus, Christ was not born in winter.

Reply to Objection 3: Recall that Palestine is not England, Russia, or Alaska. Bethlehem is situated at the latitude of 31.7. My city of Dallas, Texas has the latitude of 32.8, and it's still rather comfortable outside in December. As the great Cornelius a Lapide remarks during his lifetime, one could still see shepherds and sheep in the fields of Italy during late December, and Italy is at higher latitude than Bethlehem.

Now we move on to establishing the birthday of Christ from Sacred Scripture in two steps. The first step is to use Scripture to determine the birthday of Saint John the Baptist. The next step is using Saint John the Baptist's birthday as the key for finding Christ's birthday. We can discover that Christ was born in late December by observing first the time of year in which Saint Luke describes Saint Zacharias in the temple. This provides us with the approximate conception date of Saint John the Baptist. From there we can follow the chronology that Saint Luke gives, and that lands us at the end of December.

Saint Luke reports that Zacharias served in the "course of Abias" (Lk 1:5) which Scripture records as the eighth course among the twenty-four priestly courses (Neh 12:17). Each shift of priests served one week in the temple for two times each year. The course of Abias served during the eighth week and the thirty-second week in the annual cycle.[16] However, when did the cycle of courses begin?

Josef Heinrich Friedlieb has convincingly established that the first priestly course of Jojarib was on duty during the destruction of Jerusalem on the ninth day of the Jewish month of Av.[17] Thus the priestly course of Jojarib was on duty during the second week of Av. Consequently, the priestly course of Abias (the course of Saint Zacharias) was undoubtedly serving during the second week of the Jewish month of Tishri—the very week of the Day of Atonement on the tenth day of Tishri. In our calendar, the Day of Atonement would land anywhere from September 22 to October 8.

Zacharias and Elizabeth conceived John the Baptist immediately after Zacharias served his course. This entails that Saint John the Baptist would have been conceived somewhere around the end of September, placing John's birth at the end of June, confirming the Catholic Church's celebration of the Nativity of Saint John the Baptist on June 24.

The second-century *Protoevangelium of Saint James* also confirms a late September conception of the Baptist since the work depicts Saint Zacharias as High Priest and as entering the Holy of Holies—not merely the holy place with the altar of incense. This is a factual mistake because Zacharias was not the high priest, but one of the chief priests.[18] Still, the *Protoevangelium* regards Zacharias as a high priest and this associates him with the Day of Atonement, which lands on the tenth day of the Hebrew month of Tishri (roughly the end of our September). Immediately after this entry into the temple and message of the Archangel Gabriel, Zacharias and Elizabeth conceive John the Baptist. Allowing for forty weeks of gestation, this places the birth of John the Baptist at the end of June—once again confirming the Catholic date for the Nativity of Saint John the Baptist on June 24.

The rest of the dating is rather simple. We read that just after the Immaculate Virgin Mary conceived Christ, she went to visit her cousin Elizabeth who was six months pregnant with John the Baptist. This means that

John the Baptist was six months older that our Lord Jesus Christ (Lk 1:24-27, 36). If you add six months to June 24 you get December 24-25 as the birthday of Christ. Then, if you subtract nine months from December 25 you get that the Annunciation was March 25. All the dates match up perfectly. So then, if John the Baptist was conceived shortly after the Jewish Day of the Atonement, then the traditional Catholic dates are essentially correct. The birth of Christ would be about or on December 25.

Sacred Tradition also confirms December 25 as the birthday of the Son of God. The source of this ancient tradition is the Blessed Virgin Mary herself. Ask any mother about the birth of her children. She will not only give you the date of the birth, but she will be able to rattle off the time, the location, the weather, the weight of the baby, the length of the baby, and a number of other details. I'm the father of seven blessed children, and while I sometimes forget these details—*mea maxima culpa*—my wife never does. You see, mothers never forget the details surrounding the births of their babies.

Now ask yourself: Would the Blessed Virgin Mary ever forget the birth of her Son Jesus Christ who was conceived without human seed, proclaimed by angels, born in a miraculous way, and visited by Magi? She knew from the moment of His incarnation in her stainless womb that He was the Son of God and Messiah. Would she ever forget that day?[19]

Next, ask yourself: Would the Apostles be interested in hearing Mary tell the story? Of course they would. Do you think the holy Apostle who wrote, "And the Word was made flesh," was not interested in the minute details of His birth? Even when I walk around with our seven-month-old son, people always ask "How old is he?" or "When was he born?" Don't you think people asked this question of Mary?

So the exact birth date (December 25) and the time (midnight) would have been known in the first century. Moreover, the Apostles would have asked about it and would have, no doubt, commemorated the blessed event that both Saint Matthew and Saint Luke chronicle for us. In summary, it is completely reasonable to state that the early Christians both knew and commemorated the birth of Christ. Their source would have been His Immaculate Mother.

Further testimony reveals that the Church Fathers claimed December 25 as the Birthday of Christ *prior* to the conversion of Constantine and the Roman Empire. The earliest record of this is that Pope Saint Telesphorus (reigned A.D. 126-137) instituted the tradition of Midnight Mass on Christmas Eve. Although the *Liber Pontificalis* does not give us the date of Christmas, it assumes that the Pope was already celebrating Christmas and that a Mass at midnight was added. During this time, we also read the following words of Theophilus (A.D. 115-181), Catholic bishop of Caesarea in Palestine: "We ought to celebrate the birthday of Our Lord on what day soever the 25th of December shall happen."[20]

Shortly thereafter in the second century, Saint Hippolytus (A.D. 170-240) wrote in passing that the birth of Christ occurred on December 25:

> The First Advent of our Lord in the flesh occurred when He was born in Bethlehem, was December 25th, a Wednesday, while Augustus was in his forty-second year, which is five thousand and five hundred years from Adam. He suffered in the thirty-third year, March 25th, Friday, the eighteenth year of Tiberius Caesar, while Rufus and Roubellion were Consuls.[21]

Also note in the quote above the special significance of March 25, which marks the death of Christ (March 25 was assumed to corresponded to the Hebrew month Nisan 14 - the traditional date of crucifixion).[22] Christ, as the perfect man, was believed to have been conceived and died on the same day—March 25. In his *Chronicon*, Saint Hippolytus states that the earth was created on March 25, 5500 B.C. Thus, March 25 was identified by the Church Fathers as the Creation date of the universe, as the date of the Annunciation and Incarnation of Christ, and also as the date of the Death of Christ our Savior.

In the Syrian Church, March 25 or the Feast of the Annunciation was seen as one of the most important feasts of the entire year. It denoted the day that God took up his abode in the womb of the Virgin. In fact, if the Annunciation and Good Friday came into conflict on the calendar, the Annunciation trumped it, so important was the day in Syrian tradition. It goes without saying that the Syrian Church preserved some of the most ancient Christian traditions and had a sweet and profound devotion for Mary and the Incarnation of Christ.

Now then, March 25 was enshrined in the early Christian tradition, and from this date it is easy to discern the date of Christ's birth. March 25 (Christ conceived by the Holy Ghost) plus nine months brings us to December 25 (the birth of Christ at Bethlehem).

Saint Augustine confirms this tradition of March 25 as the Messianic conception and December 25 as His birth:

> For Christ is believed to have been conceived on the 25th of March, upon which day also he suffered; so the womb of the Virgin, in which he was conceived, where no one of mortals was begotten,

corresponds to the new grave in which he was buried, wherein was never man laid, neither before him nor since. But he was born, according to tradition, upon December the 25th.[23]

In about A.D. 400, Saint Augustine also noted how the schismatic Donatists celebrated December 25 as the birth of Christ, but that the schismatics refused to celebrate Epiphany on January 6, since they regarded Epiphany as a new feast without a basis in Apostolic Tradition. The Donatist schism originated in A.D. 311 which may indicate that the Latin Church was celebrating a December 25 Christmas (but not a January 6 Epiphany) before A.D. 311. Whichever is the case, the liturgical celebration of Christ's birth was commemorated in Rome on December 25 long before Christianity became legalized and long before our earliest record of a pagan feast for the birthday of the Unconquered Sun. For these reasons, it is reasonable and right to hold that Christ was born on December 25 in 1 B.C. and that he died and rose again in March of A.D. 33.

The Wise Men Recognize the Jewish King

A word must be said here about the Wise Men. It has often been explained by provocative preachers that Scripture does not explicitly record that there were *three* Wise Men. This is only a reasonable conclusion based on the fact that the Wise Men presented *three* gifts. It is assumed, therefore, that there were three gift-givers. The alleged relics of the *three* Wise Men rest in the Cathedral of Cologne, Germany. According to tradition, Saint Helena discovered the grave of the Wise Men and their remains were later transported to the Church of Hagia Sophia in Constantinople. Later these relics were moved to Milan before finally coming to their current resting place in A.D. 1164. However, the Milanese still celebrate the fact that these relics once resided in Milan by hosting a medieval costume parade every January 6.

Traditional iconography depicts them as representing three different races. The book of Genesis explains that Noah had three sons and that these three sons repopulated the earth. The genealogies listed in Genesis chapters ten and eleven reveal that Noah's son Shem fathered the people who would become the nations of Middle East. This includes the Israelites, and for this reason they are called *Semitic* people – from the name *Shem*. Ham, the second son of Noah, become the father of the Canaanite, Egyptian, and African peoples. Noah's third son Japheth fathered the people who eventually populated Europe.

Thus, most nativity scenes depict the Three Wise Men as representatives of these three "sons of Noah." Melchior is the "Shemite" and is typically depicted as an Arabian. Balthasar is the "Hamite" and is typically represented as a young African or Moor. Gaspar or Casper is sometimes featured as a European, at other times Far Eastern or Asian. The symbolism (which didn't fully develop until the twelfth century) points to the reality that every tribe and nation of the world has come to adore the Son of God.

Now Matthew records that the Wise Men visited the Infant Jesus in a *house*. "And going into the *house* they saw the child with Mary his mother, and they fell down and worshiped him" (Mt 2:11). Modern commentators make much of this. They suggest that Jesus, Mary, Joseph had relocated to a physical home and perhaps lived for some time in a house of Bethlehem. This is not only contrary to tradition, but it also does not make sense of the Scriptural context. "They found the Babe lying in the manger." If Joseph and Mary had relocated to an established home, why is Christ still using an animal's food trough for His bed? The answer is that Jesus, Mary, and Joseph were still living in the cave of Bethlehem, which served as a stable.

Why, then does Saint Matthew refer to a "house"? The answer is that Jews call any home a house. In Psalm 103, as Cornelius a Lapide notes, refers to a bird's nest as a "house." Francisco Suárez concludes: "It is plain that Christ, and the Blessed Virgin, as a woman who had lately given birth to a child, remained in the stable until her Purification." Saint Justin Martyr and Saint Augustine are also of the opinion that "house" in Matthew 2:11 refers to the stable in which Christ was born.[24]

After the Wise Men left Joseph received an angelic warning of Herod's impending massacre in a dream:

> Behold, an angel of the Lord appeared to Joseph in a dream and said, "Rise, take the child and his mother, and flee to Egypt, and remain there till I tell you; for Herod is about to search for the child, to destroy him." And he rose and took the child and his mother by night, and departed to Egypt (Mt 2:14-14).

So Joseph packed up once again and led the baby Messiah and his Mother into Egypt until Herod the Great should die. No doubt the costly gifts of the Wise Men helped subsidize their journey into the land of Egypt.

King Herod as Rome's Anti-Messiah

When King Herod the Great learned that a great king had been born in Bethlehem, he ordered the death of every male under the age of two within that city.

> Then Herod, when he saw that he had been tricked by the wise men, was in a furious rage, and he sent and killed all the male children in Bethlehem and in all that region who were two years old or under, according to the time which he had ascertained from the wise men (Matt. 2:16).

This tragic event is commemorated on December 28 as the feast of the Holy Innocents. It may seem hard to believe that a ruler would order the death of innocent children, but a little background information concerning Herod the Great reveals that this sort of act was in perfect keeping with his abhorrent character.

Herod the Great seized rule in Palestine by slaying some fifty leading Jewish men to ensure that his reign would remain undisputed. This number included leaders of the Sanhedrin. The Sanhedrin was the Jewish Senate of Jerusalem led by the High Priest. Herod banished his first wife Doris and their three-year-old son in order to marry the Hasmonean (that is, of the Maccabaean family dynasty) princess Mariamne. Princess Mariamne bore five children to Herod by the time she was twenty-five and then Herod killed her in a fit of jealousy. Herod the Great then murdered Princess Mariamne's parents— King Hyrcanus and Queen Alexandria. At the end of his life Herod killed his two sons Alexander and Aristobulus for fear that they might try to usurp his authority. Then five days before his death, Herod murdered another one of his sons—Antipater. Given that Herod was willing to murder his own sons out of suspicion of a rival claimant, it should be no surprise that the murderer commanded the death of all the babies in Bethlehem.

It all began when Wise Men came to Jerusalem from the East:

Now when Jesus was born in Bethlehem of Judea in the days of Herod the king, behold, wise men from the East came to Jerusalem, saying,

"Where is he who has been born king of the Jews? For we have seen his star in the East, and have come to worship him."

When Herod the king heard this, he was troubled, and all Jerusalem with him; and assembling all the chief priests and scribes of the people, he inquired of them where the Christ was to be born (Mt 2:1-4).

The star indicated that a new King of the Jews had been born. Herod had spent his entire life pulling strings in Rome and killing the suspicious for the sake of his title "King of the Jews." He was not about to give up his claim as king. Whether they knew it or not, the Wise Men were bringing very bad news to Herod the Great. A child recently born in Bethlehem had usurped the present king's authority.

Herod the Great did not get to where he was in life without a web of schemes and he wasn't going to let a defenseless baby undermine his reign. However, Herod could not kill the child if he did not know where the child was located. The Jewish scholars quoted Micah 5:2 to Herod, a commonly known passage, which states that the Messiah would be born in Bethlehem, a suburb five miles south of Jerusalem

So Herod falsely pledged his desire to pay homage to this new king and asked the Wise Men to report on the child's whereabouts. The act of Herod paying homage to this newborn king in Bethlehem would have amounted to an abdication of his status as King of the

Jews. Anyone who knew the political record of Herod the Great knew that this was not in Herod's nature.

Herod died shortly after the birth of Christ. The Jewish historian Josephus records that Herod died an excruciating death related to kidney disease and gangrene of the genitals.

> But the disease of Herod grew more severe, God inflicting punishment for his crimes. For a slow fire burned in him which was not so apparent to those who touched him, but augmented his internal distress; for he had a terrible desire for food which it was not possible to resist. He was affected also with ulceration of the intestines, and with especially severe pains in the colon, while a watery and transparent humor settled about his feet.
>
> He suffered also from a similar trouble in his abdomen. Nay more, his privy member was putrefied and produced worms. He found also excessive difficulty in breathing, and it was particularly disagreeable because of the offensiveness of the odor and the rapidity of respiration.
>
> He had convulsions also in every limb, which gave him uncontrollable strength. It was said, indeed, by those who possessed the power of divination and wisdom to explain such events, that God had inflicted this punishment upon the King on account of his great impiety.[25]

Herod had two Jewish scribes burned on the occasion of his death so that Jerusalem would be filled with mourning at his death. Instead, Jerusalem responded with a revolt during the feast of Pentecost.

Herod had left a plan of succession and Rome accordingly confirmed it. Palestine was divided into three districts to be ruled by Herod's three sons, the only ones he hadn't murdered. Archelaus became the ethnarch of Judea, Samaria, and Idumea. Herod Antipas became the tetrarch of Galilee and Perea. Herod Philip I became tetrarch of the northeastern region of Ituraea and Trachonitis. In all three cases, Rome did not grant these three sons the right to bear the title of *king*. Perhaps Rome had seen enough bloodshed. Instead, they were *rulers*.

After Herod the Great had died, an angel came once again to Joseph in a dream and informed him that Herod had died and that it was safe to return to the Holy Land. Joseph soon learned that Herod's son Archelaus had succeeded his father as ruler of Judaea. "He was afraid to go there." (Matt. 2:22) It seems that Joseph received yet another dream and "withdrew to the district of Galilee." (Matt 2:22)

Archelaus would fall into disfavor only a few years later and lived in exile for the rest of his life in what is now France. In A.D. 6, Rome combined Judea, Samaria, and Idumea to create the united Roman province of Judaea. From that time forward, the Jews were ruled directly by a series of Roman prefects. The first prefect was Coponius (A.D. 6-9), the second was Marcus Ambibulus (9-12), and the third was Annius Rufus (12-15). Valerius Gratus (15-26) was the fourth prefect of Judea, and he appointed Joseph Caiaphas as High Priest. This is the same Caiaphas who masterminded the plot against Jesus Christ. The prefect after Gratus was the most famous prefect of all time: Pontius Pilate (prefect from A.D. 26-36). Rome had tightened its grip around Judea. Meanwhile to the north, the Messiah was passing his adolescence and early manhood in the district of

Galilee. The spiritual battle for Rome and the rest of humanity had yet to be fought.

NOTES

[3] Josephus, *War of the Jews*, 14.4.

[4] Virgil applied this Cumæan prophecy to Pollio, the son of the Roman Consul Asinius Pollio. Virgil's application is incorrect and an example of flattery since Pollio's mother was neither a virgin nor from Heaven. The true fulfillment is found in Christ.

[5] Cicero, *De Divinitate*, 2, 54.

[6] Suetonius. *Vespas., c.* 4.

[7] Tacitus, *Hist.,* 5, 13.

[8] Saint Louis de Montfort relates this account in his *Secret of the Rosary*, Part 1, Sixth Rose.

[9] Quoted by Cornelius a Lapide in his *Commentary on Luke* at Luke 2:1.

[10] This tradition is confirmed by Baronius, citing Suidas, Nicephorus, and others, in the materials of his *Annals*.

[11] Hugues de Nanteuil, *Sur les dates de naissance et de mort de Jésus*, Paris: Téqui editions, 1988. Translated by J.S. Daly and F. Egregyi. Paris, 2008.

[12] de Nanteuil, 2008.

[13] Josephus, *Antiquities,* 12.

[14] Josephus, *Antiquities*, 14.

[15] *The Chronography of AD 354*. Part 12: Commemorations of the Martyrs. MGH *Chronica Minora* I (1892), pp. 71-2.

[16] I realize that there are two courses of Abias. This theory only works if Zacharias and Elizabeth conceived John the Baptist after Zacharias' second course - the

course in September. If Saint Luke refers to the first course, this then would place the birth of John the Baptist in late Fall and the birth of Christ in late Spring. However, I think tradition and the Protoevangelium substantiate that the Baptist was conceived in late September.

[17] Josef Heinrich Friedlieb's *Leben J. Christi des Erlösers*. Münster, 1887, p. 312.

[18] The Greek tradition especially celebrates Saint Zacharias as "high priest." Nevertheless, Acts 5:24 reveals that there were several "chief priests" (ἀρχιερεῖς), and thus the claim that Zacharias was a "high priest" may not indicate a contradiction. The Greek tradition identifies Zacharias as an archpriest and martyr based on the narrative of the Protoevangelium of James and Matthew 23:35: "That upon you may come all the just blood that hath been shed upon the earth, from the blood of Abel the just, even unto the blood of Zacharias the son of Barachias, whom you killed between the temple and the altar." (Matthew 23:35)

[19] A special thanks to the Reverend Father Phil Wolfe, FSSP for bringing the "memory of Mary" argument to my attention.

[20] *Magdeburgenses*, Cent. 2. c. 6. Hospinian, *De origine Festorum Chirstianorum.*

[21] Saint Hippolytus of Rome, *Commentary on Daniel.*

[22] There is some discrepancy in the Fathers as to whether Nisan 14/March 25 marked the death of Christ or his resurrection.

[23] Saint Augustine, *De trinitate,* 4, 5.

[24] Saint Augustine, *Sermones* 1 & 2 de Epiph. Saint Justin Martyr, *Against Trypho.*

[25] Josephus, *Antiquities,* 17.6.5

4. Crucified under Pontius Pilate

The shape of the cross extending out into four extremes from their central point of contact denotes the power and the providence diffused everywhere of Him who hung upon it.

- Saint Gregory of Nyssa[26]

OUR LORD JESUS CHRIST was born in Bethlehem according to the prophecy of Micah. He spent his infancy in Egypt. The majority of His life was spent in Galilee. Christ would have gone with family to Jerusalem for the great Jewish feasts, but otherwise he was occupied in Galilee. We read of no miracles during his youth, only of a single instance in which Mary and Joseph find Him in the Temple after three days of disappearance. Afterward, Jesus returned to Nazareth with Mary and Joseph, and "was obedient to them" (Lk 2:51). Nothing more is said. These are the hidden years.

In the first chapter, we learned how the Book of Daniel describes that "the Son of Man" will appear during the era of the Fourth Kingdom, that is the Roman Empire, and that He would receive a "kingdom that shall not be destroyed" (Daniel 7:13-14). In the ninth chapter of the Book of Daniel we learn that the *Messiah* shall appear 483 years from the commission to rebuild in 456 B.C. (Dan. 9:20-27). From these two prophecies we learn two things: A) that the Messiah would come during the reign of the Fourth Kingdom, and B) that the Messiah shall appear in A.D. 30.

It is precisely these two prophecies that cause so much consternation for Orthodox Jews. The Book of Daniel is obviously a book of prophecy, but the early Rabbis rejected it as a prophetic work. Instead of assigning it a place with the Prophets (e.g. Isaiah, Jeremiah, Ezekiel), they place it with the Writings (e.g. Proverbs). Daniel is obviously a work of prophecy, but Jewish scholars have difficulty with its prophecy.

The most widely accepted medieval Jewish scholar Rabbi Moses ben Maimon, or Maimonides, acknowledged that the Book of Daniel *seems to have predicted* that the Messiah would appear some time *before* A.D. 70. However, Maimonides does not believe that the Messiah came in the first century. So he was stuck with a problem: How could Daniel predict that the Messiah would come in the first half of the first century if the Messiah in fact never appeared? Maimonides simply states, "We cannot assert that Daniel was wrong in his reckoning," and instead teaches that it is a sin to try to calculate the prophecy of Daniel![27]

In the nineteenth century, two Jewish brothers tackled this problem head-on. The Lemann brothers were twins who had been orphaned at an early age. Nevertheless, their aristocratic Jewish family in Lyons raised them according to the precepts of rabbinical Judaism. As they studied the Old Testament prophecies of Daniel concerning the time of the coming Messiah, they came to this conclusion:

> Then, we said to ourselves 'If the Messiah has already come, it is Jesus Christ, and we must become Christians. If he has not yet come, we must nevertheless no longer remain Jews, because the time of the

promise has passed, and our books have lied.'[28]

The Lemann brothers acknowledged that, "the time of promise has passed." Either Jesus Christ was the promised Messiah or the Jewish Scriptures were fraudulent. The twin brothers received baptism and both became Catholic priests.[29] The consternation of Maimonides and the conversion of the Lemann's over the Book of Daniel's dating of the Messiah show that the Book of Daniel is the Achilles' heel of Rabbinical Judaism. Either Daniel was right and the Messiah has already come, or the Book of Daniel contains false prophecy. According to the Torah, any prophet that speaks falsely in the name of the Lord is condemned (cf. Deut. 18:20-22).

The Book of Daniel shows that the coming of the Messiah was synchronized with the coming of the Roman Empire. The Christian understands that the Messiah was Jesus of Nazareth, and the Catholic Christian also understands the Roman features of the birth, death, and resurrection of the Messiah. In the previous chapter we examined how the Messiah was born in Bethlehem because the Roman Caesar issued a decree that census should be taken. In this chapter we examine the role of the Roman Prefect of Judea in the death of the Messiah.

Rome had instituted the three men that condemned Our Lord Jesus Christ. Antipas ruled over Galilee, Pontius Pilate ruled over Judea, and Joseph Caiaphas served as the High Priest in Jerusalem. These three men did not like one another, and each of them had different ideas as to how Palestine should be ruled. Oddly enough the Messiah united them in a common cause.

The Jewish Divisions under Roman Rule

There were also quarrelling factions beneath these three rulers. As we discussed in the second chapter, two major parties emerged after Maccabaean revolt, the Pharisees and the Sadducees. The Pharisees were the Jewish Puritans of the day. Pharisees sought the coming of the Messiah and the resurrection of the dead. Their faith was a daily affair that touched every detail of their lives. The Sadducees accepted only the first five books of the Scriptures and understood the Jewish faith primarily in priestly and sacrificial terms.

There were of course other sects. There were the Samaritans in Samaria. They were half-breed Jews who had built their own Temple on Mount Gerizim. The Samaritan woman confirms this tradition in her conversation with Christ:

> Our fathers worshiped on this mountain [Mount Gerizim], and you say that in Jerusalem is the place where men ought to worship (Jn 4:20).

During the troublesome times of Antiochus IV Epiphanes, the Samaritans sent a letter of concord to the Greeks and agreed to have their temple on Mt. Gerizim dedicated to *Zeus, Father of the Greeks*. John Hyrcanus destroyed the Samaritan Temple on Mount Gerizim in about 128 B.C. This action and the paganism of the Samarians led to the final and lasting estrangement between the Samaritans and the Jews as indicated in John 4:9, "For Jews have no dealings with Samaritans."

There were also the Essenes. Josephus and Philo testify that the Essenes were Jews leading a communal life of celibacy. Josephus also mentions a secondary rank of Essences who did marry. They abstained from meat and also from the religious animal sacrifices of the

Temple. Josephus records that Essenes endured a three-year novitiate before taking formal vows. Like the Pharisees, they believed in the immortality of the soul, the existence of angels, and life after death. They also seemed to have performed daily ceremonial washings. Some scholars have sought to find the origins of Christianity with the Essene movement. Many have sought to identify John the Baptist as the quintessential ascetic character of an Essene, who also popularized the ritual washing of baptism. The Essenes cannot be categorically associated with Christianity because the sect continued to exist as a separate movement as late as the fourth century A.D.[30]

Lastly, there were the "Herodians." The Herodians are mentioned frequently as a party that opposed Christ during His ministry in Galilee and Jerusalem (Mt 22:16; Mk 3:6; 8:15 12:13; Lk 13:31-32). Unlike the Pharisees, Sadducees, Samaritans, and Essenes, they are not a religious sect but a political party. As their name indicates, they are supporters of Herod the Great and his successors. They are what we might call today the "liberal secularists." The Herodians knew that Rome had grown strong and that future success lay in aligning with the political power of Rome and their puppet rulers of Palestine—the Herods. Any Jew that had been a tax collector would have likely been a Herodian (for example, Saint Matthew before his vocation). If the Herodians did have a religious attachment, it would have been to the Sadducees. The Sadducees were "institution men" and grateful to King Herod the Great for having revitalized Jerusalem and the Temple. The Sadducees were therefore more tolerant of the Roman occupation of Jerusalem. Roman rule through the person of Herod allowed the Sadducees to stay in power. This is one reason why we hear them shouting to Pilate, "We have no king but Caesar" (Jn 19:15).

This was the religious and political landscape during the time of Christ. Rome dominated the scene and the Jews had their various ways of dealing with it. The Pharisees pursued purity in expectation of Messianic deliverance. The Sadducees treasured the Temple and kept their heads down. The Essenes contemplated the apocalypse when all would be set right, and the Herodians just rode the wave of Roman success. Nevertheless, every believing Jew held the conviction that the kingdom should be ruled by the successor of King David. Instead, a pagan Caesar living on the Italian peninsula ruled over them. Having read the prophet Daniel, the Jews would have expected a time of heathen domination over the Jews, but they also eagerly expected God to intervene and establish His glorious kingdom.

Just at this time, John the Baptist began to preach, "The Kingdom of God is at hand" (Mt 3:2). John the Baptist could have said a lot of other things such as "Love your neighbor" or "Have faith in God." No, John the Baptist began to preach the most provocative message imaginable. He proclaimed a message about the *Kingdom*.

The Herodians did not appreciate this message because it upset the political status quo. Moreover, John the Baptist had some things to say about the adulterous marriage of Herod Antipas. The Sadducees were likely alarmed because John the Baptist was a priest who had rejected the Temple for the desert. You would think that the Pharisees would have flocked to John, but they also avoided him. This was because John told the Pharisees (as well as the Sadducees) that they were part of the problem—that they were hypocrites. The only way to prepare for the Kingdom of God was to repent, and a Jew visibly signified this repentance by baptism.

Jesus as the Son of Man under Roman Rule

John's baptism was radical. This is something we miss because modern readers do not appreciate the redemptive history of Israel. John's baptism was significant because it occurred in the Jordan River. The Jordan River was the entry point of Israel into the Holy Land under the leadership of Joshua. When the Israelites crossed through the Jordan River, the Kingdom of God had entered into Palestine. John the Baptist is now calling Jews to return to their origins; to purify themselves by re-entering the Holy Land; to bring the Kingdom of God back into Palestine. Just as Joshua established the Kingdom of God by leading the Israelites into Palestine, so another divinely appointed leader would lead Israel to reestablish the Kingdom of God once again.

Then it happened. A man stepped forward to receive baptism and a dove descended upon Him. A voice from Heaven was heard to say, "This is my beloved Son, with whom I am well pleased" (Mt 3:17). A new Joshua had appeared to re-establish the Kingdom of God. And wouldn't you know it, His name was also Joshua, for *Jesus* is merely the Greek form of the Hebrew name *Joshua*. The year was A.D. 30—the year prophesied by the Book of Daniel.

Jesus begins his three-year ministry with the same proclamation of John the Baptist: "Repent for the Kingdom of God is at hand." This is a threatening political message. Not only does Jesus continue to speak about the Kingdom (His parables are almost solely dedicated to the topic), but He also begins to identify Himself as the prophetic Son of Man.

There came one like the Son of Man,
and he came to the Ancient of Days
and was presented before him.
And to him was given dominion

and glory and kingdom (Dan 7:13-14).

In his proclamation of the Gospel, the Lord Jesus Christ presents Himself as the Son of Man ready to establish the Kingdom of God foretold by the prophet Daniel.

Christ's three-year ministry encompassed three different Passovers, on the last of which He died only to rise three days later. During this time He prepared His Apostles to announce the Kingdom that He had inaugurated. This Kingdom was not merely a national Jewish kingdom, it was the universal kingdom envisioned by Daniel. It was for Jews and for Gentiles.

This message threatened Herod Antipas who was happily ruling over his slice of Palestine. Christ's new Kingdom threatened the Roman domination represented by Pontius Pilate. He threatened the priestly caste of the Temple who saw in Christ a competitor, not a Savior. The Pharisees rejected Him because He made Himself out to be greater than the Law and the Prophets. So in spite of all their differences and squabbles, they united for one purpose and one purpose only – to rid the world of Jesus of Nazareth. This would prove to be an impossible task, because not even death could hold Him.

By the Passover in the year A.D. 33 Christ was thirty-three years old. The Sunday previous, he rode into Jerusalem with people shouting, "Hosanna to the Son of David!" Their expected Messiah had arrived. By Wednesday, Judas had gone to the High Priest, Joseph Caiaphas, and arranged to betray Him. On Thursday evening Christ sat at Passover with His Apostles and instituted the Sacrament of His Body and Blood. Afterward, Judas betrayed Him, and by morning He was standing before the Roman prefect Pontius Pilate.

Why did the Jews bring Jesus to Pontius Pilate? Pilate himself seemed perplexed by the Jewish insistence that he judge Jesus:

> So Pilate went out to them and said, "What accusation do you bring against this man? Take him yourselves and judge him by your own law."

> The Jews said to him, "It is not lawful for us to put any man to death."

Pilate was aware that the Jews did judge and kill others. We know that the Pharisees were ready to stone the woman caught in adultery (Jn 8:3-4). Later, they openly stoned Saint Stephen to death (Acts 7:57-60). At one point they took up stones and were ready to kill Jesus, but He escaped (Jn 10:31-39). Why did not the Jewish leaders of the time simply take up stones and kill Jesus?

The answer is found in Luke 22:2 where we learn that "the chief priests and the scribes were seeking how to put him to death, because they feared the people." Jesus was different from an adulteress or simple disciple like Stephen. Christ had a huge following. Palm Sunday revealed that Christ had become more than just a celebrated Rabbi. He was not only popular, but He was threatening. His teachings challenged the claim of the Pharisees, Sadducees, and Herodians. The chief priests knew that if they stoned Jesus, the people would revolt against them. They desired to arrange that the Roman establishment might sentence Jesus to death, and there was only one charge that they could lay against Him — that Jesus had claimed to possess royal authority against the claims of Rome.

Pilate entered the praetorium and summoned Jesus into his presence and asked Him, "Are you the King of the Jews?" As we discussed previously, the title of "King of the Jews" had not been known since the birth of Christ. Herod the Great was the last man to possess it, and he died less than a few years after he decreed the murder of the innocent children in Bethlehem. At that point Rome retired the title "King of the Jews." Herod's sons were called only *ethnarch* or *tetrarch*. The Jewish leaders charged that Christ had taken up the title of Herod the Great. So Pilate asked Jesus, "Are you the King of the Jews?"

Jesus answered, "Do you say this of your own accord, or did others say it to you about me?" In other words, Jesus wants to know, "Did you come up with this yourself or are the Jews trying to use you to get to me?"

Pilate revealed that he is a no-nonsense Italian administrator. "Am I a Jew? Your own nation and the chief priests have handed you over to me. What have you done?" Pilate speaks straight. It is as if Pilate said, "The priests have put me up to this. Have you really done anything wrong?"

Echoing the imagery of Daniel, Christ explained that the His Kingdom is made, "by no human hand" and is therefore, "not from this world" (see Jn 18:36; Dan 2:44-45). Pilate pounced on the word *kingdom* and asks, "So you are a king?" Jesus answered, "You say that I am a king. For this I was born, and for this I have come into the world, to bear witness to the truth. Everyone who is of the truth hears my voice" (Jn 18:37). Pilate responded, "What is truth?" We do not know if Pilate said this in a cynical tone or in a sincere tone. Regardless, he had heard enough to know that Jesus was innocent. He went out to the hostile Jewish leaders and announced:

> I find no crime in him. But you have a custom that I should release one man for you at the Passover. Will you have me release for you the King of the Jews? They cried out again, "Not this man, but

Barabbas!" Now Barabbas was a robber (Jn 18:38-40).

It seems that Pilate was testing the Jewish leaders. He gave them a chance to have Jesus declared guilty but then also released. However, the Jewish leaders wanted Jesus nailed to a cross. There would be no compromise. They ask for Barabbas. We do not know much about Barabbas, but his name is striking. In Aramaic the name *Bar-Abbas* means "Son of the Father." They wrongly ask for a criminal, a false *son of the father* in exchange for the true *Son of the Father*.

Pilate tries a second test. He has Christ scourged at the pillar. He then has Jesus crowned with thorns and robed in purple. He presents Christ before them, bloody and beaten. "Behold, the man!" Yet the Jewish leaders are not content. Instead they cry out, "Crucify him! Crucify him!"

> Pilate answered, "Take him yourselves and crucify him, for I find no crime in him." The Jews answered him, "We have a law, and by that law he ought to die, because he has made himself the Son of God." When Pilate heard these words, he was the more afraid (Jn 19:6-8).

Pilate was "more afraid." What did he fear? Perhaps this sober Roman official recognized something unique in the eyes of Christ. Pilate returned to Jesus and asked:

> "Where are you from?"

> But Jesus gave no answer. Pilate therefore said to him, "You will not speak to me? Do you not know that I have power to release you, and power to crucify you?"

> Jesus answered him, "You would have no power over me unless it had been given you from above; therefore, he who delivered me to you has the greater sin."

> Upon this Pilate sought to release him, but the Jews cried out, "If you release this man, you are not Caesar's friend; everyone who makes himself a king sets himself against Caesar" (Jn 19:9-12).

Christ's answer reveals the tension between the Roman Empire and the Kingdom of Heaven. Christ our Lord says, "You would have no power over me unless it had been given you from above." Christ tells Pilate that Rome only exists because "it had been given you from above." Just as Augustus Caesar played a part in the birthplace of Christ, so now God has appointed this Roman prefect to play a part in the death of Christ.

The Jews make a new argument against Pilate. "If you release this man, you are not Caesar's friend." The Jewish leaders are no longer appealing to their own laws and traditions. They are playing politics. All of the Jewish leaders want an independent Jewish kingdom, but they'd rather serve Caesar than Christ.

> When Pilate heard these words, he brought Jesus out and sat down on the judgment seat at a place called The Pavement...He said to the Jews, "Behold your King!"

> They cried out, "Away with him, away with him, crucify him!"

> Pilate said to them, "Shall I crucify your King?"

> The chief priests answered, "We have no king but Caesar."

> Then he handed him over to them to be crucified.
> (Jn 19:13-16)

These last words of the chief priests are the *most* blasphemous words ever uttered by a Jew. "We have no king but Caesar." It would be tantamount to Jews in the days of David saying, "We have no king but Goliath!" This claim of "no king but Caesar" indicates the final apostasy of the priestly leadership of Jerusalem. To use the words of the Apocalypse, they had become the Whore of Babylon, aligned not with God's covenant, but with the idolatrous super-power of Rome. Within a few short hours, Jesus would be hanging on a *Roman* cross under the words "King of the Jews" written in three languages: Hebrew, Greek, and *Latin*. They had exchanged God and the Davidic monarchy for the idolatrous emperor of Rome. The High Priests had submitted not to the God of Israel, but to the monstrous fourth Beast described by Daniel.

Roman Crucifixion

The everlasting sacrifice for the redemption of mankind occurred not on the ancient altar of burnt offerings standing in the Holy Temple of Jerusalem — but on the hard wood of a Roman cross. The blood of the Messiah ran down the instrument of punishment favored by the powerful Roman legions.

Almost every ancient culture employed a form of capital punishment that involved impaling the body of a victim on a pole. The Assyrians, Egyptians, Persians, and Greeks all practiced a form of impalement. It is not clear from historical records whether the victims were already dead when they were impaled or whether they died by way of impalement. It is likely that both living and dead bodies were publicly impaled. The intent is to proclaim to the public that the enemy is dead and humiliated.

The Roman Empire, however, had developed impalement into something worse. They did not wish to merely display a dead body or quickly kill a victim by poking a hole through him atop a pole. The Roman word for the cross was *crux*, which originally denoted only a wooden stake and not what we now identify with a cross. Crucifixion before the time of Christ was simply the ancient custom of *arbori impalare* ("impalement on a tree"). The Roman author Seneca the Younger (ca. 4 B.C.—65 A.D.) speaks of the *infelix lignum* ("unlucky wood") on which a victim is seated on a sharp wooden pike.[31] This kind of "crucifixion" corresponds to the Assyrian and Carthaginian custom of impaling victims through the anus, the effect of which was a swift and painful death on account of the terrible amount of hemorrhaging.

As terrible as this may sound, the Romans developed crucifixion into an even more excruciating form of torture. I must pause here as I write simply to say that the word used in the previous sentence *excruciating*, has entered into English from the Latin word for cross: *crux*. Excruciation is the pain that comes from the cross. The Romans succeeded in making their *crux* even more *excruciating*. It is terrible to be impaled through the anus, but it is much worse to be nailed through the non-vital appendages of the body so that one lives for as long as several days under the weight of one's own body. Heat, rain, cold, sunburn, birds, thirst, hunger—each compounded the torture of Roman crucifixion. This form of crucifixion was a slow torture, killing the victim over a period of days by suffocation. The crucified slowly lost blood through the small wounds in his wrists and feet and through dehydration. The diminished blood supply caused the vital organs (primarily the diaphragm and heart) to fail, and the victim died. Typically the body was left on the cross as carrion for vultures and birds.

Romans acknowledged this kind of crucifixion to be the most disgraceful form of death, and it was reserved only for slaves, traitors, and other public enemies of the Roman Empire. Roman citizens, no matter how traitorous, were exempt from crucifixion. We observe this historical distinction in the deaths of Saint Peter and Saint Paul. As we will discuss in the next chapter, Saint Peter was not a Roman citizen, and he died by crucifixion. Saint Paul was a Roman citizen, and he died "honorably" by decapitation.

Mass crucifixions were sometimes ordered in the case of rebellions. The slave rebellion of Spartacus in 71 B.C. led to the mass crucifixion of over 6,000 of his followers all along the Appian Way from Capua to Rome. The bodies remained on their crosses for years – a chilling reminder of the fate of Roman rebels. In Chapter 6, we will discuss the Roman destruction of Jerusalem during which the Romans crucified countless Jews all along the walls of the city. The Jewish historian Josephus recounts that the Roman soldiers crucified their victims in various positions for amusement. The Romans, however, often offended their own depraved sensibilities and broke the victim's legs in order to hasten death. Once they broke the legs of the crucified, he could no longer push himself upward – an action necessary to allow air into the lungs. He suffocated within minutes.

There were other ways to quicken the death of the crucified. If the Romans scourged their victim prior to his crucifixion, the victim would lose large amounts of blood, blood necessary to carry oxygen to the body's organs. Suffocation would come sooner rather than later. Sometimes the victim was humiliated to the point of carrying his own cross. In most cases, the victim carried only the *patibulum* ("horizontal beam") of the cross. This beam would then be attached to a vertical post, usually a designated tree that had been stripped of its limbs.

Why a Roman Cross?

Some Christians have been confused because Sacred Scripture sometimes refers to Christ as having been nailed to a tree and not to a cross.

"Jesus whom you killed by hanging him on a tree" (Acts 5:30).

"Cursed be he who hangs on a tree" (Gal 3:13).

"He himself bore our sins in his body on the tree" (1 Pet 2:24).

There is no contradiction here. As was often the case, the Romans would choose a suitable tree in a convenient location and strip it of its limbs so that it would be a large wooden beam extending from the earth. Moreover, there was a very important reason for using trees – it meant less work for the Roman legionaries! The tree's root system provided perfect stability for multiple crucifixions.

Once a tree was so prepared, the Romans would then place the *patibulum* ("horizontal beam") in a carved-out notch in the tree. The Greek word used in the Gospels to describe the "cross" carried by Christ is *stauros* and this term likely refers to the horizontal beam that the Romans identified as the *patibulum*. Once Christ arrived at Golgotha, this horizontal beam would have been placed into the notch of the stripped tree. The Romans would nail the victim, stripped of his clothes, to the wood and leave him to die.

Paul, the Jewish Rabbi turned Christian Apostle, explains that Christ's placement on "a tree" relates to the Law of Moses. Deuteronomy 21:23 states that the curse of God falls on any man who "hangs on a tree." Paul believes that Christ bore "the curse of the Law" through crucifixion and interprets the crucifixion in this way:

> Christ redeemed us from the curse of the law, having become a curse for us — for it is written, "Cursed be everyone who hangs on a tree" - that in Christ Jesus the blessing of Abraham might come upon the Gentiles, that we might receive the promise of the Spirit through faith (Gal. 3:13-14).

Hanging on the cross, "Christ redeemed us from the curse of the law, having become a curse for us." Paul further developed this line of thought in his stunning distilment of the Christian Gospel in 2 Corinthians 5:21:

> "For our sake he made him to be sin who knew no sin, so that in him we might become the righteousness of God."

The idea that Christ was placed "on a tree" is therefore integral to the early Church's understanding of redemption as it relates to the precepts of the Old Covenant. It is all the more striking that the Jewish leaders desired for Christ to be crucified. The priests, scribes, and Pharisees knew that crucifixion or "hanging a man on a tree" was strictly forbidden by the Old Testament because it "defiled the land which the LORD your God gives you." (Deut 21:23) Jewish law only allowed death by stoning, burning, strangulation, and decapitation. The Jewish leaders knew that only Pontius

Pilate could have given the order to nail Christ to a cross.

Saint Paul distilled his ministry with these words: "For I decided to know nothing among you except Jesus Christ and him crucified." (1 Cor 2:2) If we also desire to know Christ and Him crucified, then we know Him as nailed to the Roman cross. The most recognized symbol of Christianity is a Roman symbol. Why is Catholicism *Roman*? It is because human redemption is found traced upon the shape of the cross. The inhuman sign of Roman execution has been transformed into the life-giving source of every imaginable grace. The cross recalls not only the Christ who hung there for our redemption, but also the Roman occupation of Palestine that made the event possible.

Even so, this terrible form of Roman crucifixion was practiced for three hundred years after the death of Christ. Constantine the Great, the first Roman Emperor to officially acknowledge Christ and receive baptism, finally abolished crucifixion in honor of his Lord Jesus Christ. The story of how Constantine became a Christian is another chapter in our books. However, before getting there we must first examine how Christianity came to be established in the very city of Rome. How then did God crush the heathen Fourth Kingdom of Rome with a stone sent from Heaven, as prophesied by Daniel? The Son of Man commissioned an envoy to whom He gave the title of *Rock* or *Peter*.

NOTES

[26] Saint Gregory of Nyssa, *First Oration on the Resurrection*.

[27] Maimonides, *Igeret Teiman*, 3, 24.

NOTES CONTINUED

[28] Lemann Brothers, *Letter to the Editor*, September 17, 1854.

[29] The Lemann brothers proposed the following *Postulatum* to Pope Pius IX at the First Vatican Council (1870): "The undersigned Fathers of the Council humbly yet urgently beseechingly pray that the Holy Ecumenical Council of the Vatican deign to come to the aid of the unfortunate nation of Israel with an entirely paternal invitation; that is, that it express the wish that, finally exhausted by a wait no less futile than long, the Israelites hasten to recognize the Messiah, our Savior Jesus Christ, truly promised to Abraham and announced by Moses; thus completing and crowning, not changing, the Mosaic religion.

"On one hand, the undersigned Fathers have the very firm confidence that the holy Council will have compassion on the Israelites, because they are always very dear to God on account of their fathers, and because it is from them that the Christ was born according to the flesh.

"On the other hand, the same Fathers share the sweet and intimate hope that this ardent desire of tenderness and honor will be, with the aid of the Holy Spirit, well received by many of the sons of Abraham, because the obstacles which have held them back until now appear to be disappearing more and more, the ancient wall of separation now having fallen.

"Would that they then speedily acclaim the Christ, saying 'Hosanna to the Son of David! Blessed be He who comes in the name of the Lord!'

"Would that they hurl themselves into the arms of the Immaculate Virgin Mary, even now their sister according to the flesh, who wishes likewise to be their mother according to grace as she is ours!"

NOTES CONTINUED

[30] Saint Epiphanius, *Panarion* 1:19.
[31] *Epistulae Morales ad Lucilium*, 101:12.

5. DID PETER ESTABLISH THE CHURCH OF ROME?

The City which thou seest no other deem
Then great and glorious Rome, Queen of the Earth
So far renown'd, and with the spoils enricht
Of Nations; there the Capitol thou seest,
Above the rest lifting his stately head

The words of Satan to Christ
John Milton *Paradise Regain'd*

JUST AS ROME HAD once invaded the city of Jerusalem, so now a Jewish fisherman entered the city of Rome and changed it forever. We speak of Simon Peter, the Rock on which Christ constructed His Church. Years before Christ died on a Roman cross outside the walls of Jerusalem, He appointed twelve Apostles. He first chose Andrew and then his brother Simon who became Peter. Next he called the brothers James and John. And then he called Philip and Nathaniel. Matthew the tax collector was next. Then he called five others: Thomas, another James, another Simon, and two Judases—Judas (or Jude) Thaddeus and Judas Iscariot the betrayer.

Of these twelve, Christ chose three to form His inner circle: Simon Peter and the brothers James and John. These three Apostles were allowed to witness the raising of the daughter of Jairus, the Transfiguration of Christ on Mount Tabor, and were the three commissioned to keep vigil with Christ during His agony in the Garden of Gethsemane.

Within this apostolic triumvirate, Christ further designated one of them to a singular office. According to the Gospel of Matthew, Peter was the "first" or "chief" of the Apostles (10:2). Peter's preeminent role can be discovered from a simple statistical analysis of the New Testament. Peter's name is mentioned *more than twice as many times* as all the other disciples *combined.* Peter is mentioned 191 times in the New Testament, 162 times as Peter, twenty-three times as Simon, and six times as Cephas—the Aramaic form of Peter. The other Apostles are mentioned 130 times, but Peter alone is mentioned 191 times. Moreover, Peter's name is always the first name whenever the Apostles are listed.[32]

Certain non-Catholic scholars have challenged the Catholic claim that Peter was somehow the chief Apostle, suggesting that the Apostles were strictly egalitarian in their governance of the Church. There are a number of scriptural examples that present Saint Peter as the chief Apostle in Jerusalem after the Ascension of Christ.

1. Peter makes arrangements for the replacement for Judas Iscariot (Acts 1:15-22).
2. Peter proclaims the first public resurrection sermon to the Jews on Pentecost (Acts 2:14-36).
3. The Jews of Jerusalem regarded Peter as the leader and spokesman for the new community of Christians (Acts 4:1-13).
4. Peter pronounces the Church's first anathema against Ananias and Sapphira, an act physically confirmed by God's intervention (Acts 5:2-11).

5. Peter's shadow effects miracles (Acts 5:15).

6. Peter is the first to condemn the heresy of Simon Magus (Acts 8:14-24).

7. Peter is the first person to raise the dead (Acts 9:40).

8. Peter receives a revelation from God and is the first to admit Gentiles into the Church (Acts 10:9-48, 11:5-17).

9. The entire Church of Jerusalem offers "earnest prayer" for Peter when he is imprisoned (Acts 12:5).

10. Peter convenes and presides over Apostolic Council in Jerusalem (Acts 15:7-11).

These examples reveal that Peter held the preeminent position in Jerusalem—so much so that Paul paid a visit to Peter at the beginning of his own ministry in order to confirm the gospel he had been preaching (Gal 1:18). However, the Book of Acts does not represent Peter performing his apostolic leadership within the city of Rome. Sacred Scripture describes Peter as operating in Jerusalem. It would seem that the Church of Jerusalem, not the Church of Rome, is the original headquarters of the Church. The burden of proof for this book is to demonstrate that Christ intended for Saint Peter to transfer that headquarters from Jerusalem to Rome. Christ's intention for Peter to go to Rome is found in the Scriptural passage describing Christ's commission of Peter as His imperial vicar.

Peter became the imperial vicar of Christ when he received a new name from Christ. This new name was *Kepha* in Aramaic and *Petros* in Greek. Both words mean "rock." The reception of a new name has its roots in the Old Testament. God changed the name of Abram to Abraham. A name change symbolizes that the recipient of the new name has received a new identity from God.

Why then did Christ give Simon the name of *Rock*? To understand this mystery, we must look at Christ's words in context. Half way through the public ministry of Christ, many people began to speculate about the identity of Jesus. This is the perennial question posed to those investigating the claims of Christ. Who is Jesus?

> Now when Jesus came into the district of Caesarea Philippi, he asked his disciples, "Who do men say that the Son of Man is?"
>
> And they said, "Some say John the Baptist, others say Elijah, and others Jeremiah or one of the prophets" (Mt 16:13-14).

The Apostles had consulted the polls and generated options. Either the Son of Man was (1) John the Baptist raised from the dead, (2) Elijah the Prophet, (3) Jeremiah the Prophet, or (4) Some other Old Testament prophet.

Christ then made the question a personal one, "But who do you say that I am?" Ultimately, this is the question that Christ asks of every person who encounters Him. "Who do you think that I am?" No one but Simon spoke up:

> "You are the Christ, the Son of the living God."
>
> And Jesus answered him, "Blessed are you, Simon Bar-Jona! For flesh and blood has not revealed this to you, but my Father who is in heaven. And I tell you, you are Peter, and on this Rock I will build my church, and the powers of death shall not prevail against it. I will give you the keys of the kingdom of heaven, and whatever you bind on earth shall be bound in heaven, and whatever you loose on earth shall be loosed in heaven" (Mt 16:16-20).

Simon answered correctly. He identified Jesus as not only the Messiah but also as the Son of God. Jesus responded by giving Peter a new identity. In the original Greek text of Matthew, Jesus said, "You are *petros* and on this *petra* I will build my Church."

Protestant polemicists have often objected to the Catholic interpretation of this passage by stating that Christ made a distinction between Simon *Petros,* a masculine noun, and *petra* a feminine noun. They say that *petros* in Greek means "small stone," and that the Greek word *petra* means, "rock." Thus they say that Christ did not intend to build the Church on the "little man" of Peter but on the "great confession" of Peter's faith. Therefore, the Protestant concludes that the rock of the Church cannot refer to Peter.

It is true that *petros* means "stone" and *petra* means "rock." However, there is a very simple reason for why Matthew's Gospel made the distinction. The Greek word *petra* is feminine, and the rules of grammar prevent it from being applied to a male as a name. Moreover, Christ was *not* speaking Greek, but Aramaic. In Aramaic the word for "rock" is *kepha*, and it is not feminine. Christ would have said, "You are *kepha*, and on this *kepha* I will build my Church." There is nothing in Aramaic to distinguish the first occurrence of *kepha* from the second. The Greek text of Matthew requires the masculine/feminine distinction or *petros* and *petra* in order to preserve the pun. Moreover, Peter's identity as *Kepha* is found throughout the New Testament. Saint Paul refers to Peter eight times as *Kephas* – a Greek transliteration of the Aramaic word *Kepha*.[33] It seems that Christ named Peter with the Aramaic word for rock (*Kepha)* and that this name was later translated into Greek on account of its importance (*Petros*).

But Christ does not simply give Simon a new name. Jesus gives him something more: the keys of the kingdom. Here we have a pairing of the image of the Rock with the Kingdom of Heaven. From where does this imagery derive? The Book of Daniel.

> And in the days of those kings the God of heaven will set up a *kingdom* which shall never be destroyed, nor shall its sovereignty be left to another people. It shall break in pieces all these kingdoms and bring them to an end, and it shall stand for ever; just as you saw that a *stone* was cut from a mountain by no human hand and that it broke in pieces the iron, the bronze, the clay, the silver, and the gold (Dan 2:44-45, emphasis added).

According to the Prophet Daniel, "the God of heaven will set up a kingdom," by sending forth a "stone" to break up the Fourth Kingdom, which is Rome. That stone shall become, "a great mountain and fill the whole earth" (Dan 2:35).

When Christ appoints Simon as Peter the *Rock* and gives him the keys of the *Kingdom*, He is effectively saying that Daniel's prophecy concerning the coming of the Son of Man during the reign of the Fourth Kingdom is being fulfilled. The entire episode of Peter receiving the keys of the kingdom begins with Christ's question, "Who do men say that the Son of man is?" (Mt 16:13). Daniel identifies "the Son of Man" with the era of the Fourth Kingdom (Dan 7:13, 19).

At this point, one must ask: "This sounds nice, but it would be even better if you could prove that the word for 'rock' spoken of by Daniel is the same word used by Christ. Is *kepha* or *petra* the word used by Daniel to describe the 'stone' that crashes into the Fourth Kingdom?" This is a difficult question to answer. We are essentially dealing with three different languages: Hebrew, Aramaic, and Greek. The Book of Daniel uses the Hebrew word *eben* to describe this supernatural stone. Christ, originally speaking in Aramaic used the word *kepha*. Lastly, the Gospel of Matthew is written in Greek and uses the Greek word *petros* and *petra*. There is no way to make an absolute linguistic match. However, each maintains a dynamic equivalence with the other words. The Hebrew word *eben*, the Aramaic *kepha*, and the Greek *petros/petra* all signify the same thing: a rock or stone.[34]

It is strange that Christ would identify another man as the Rock. God is often referred to as the Rock of Israel.

> He is the Rock, his work is perfect (Deut 32:4).

> There is none holy like the LORD, there is none besides thee; there is no rock like our God (1 Sam 2:2).

> The LORD is my rock, and my fortress, and my deliverer, my God, my rock, in whom I take refuge (Ps 18:2).

> I say to God, my rock (Ps 42:9).

> Is there a God besides me? There is no Rock. I know not any (Is 44:8).

Rock, therefore, is a divine name. Peter would later identify Christ as the rock or stone of salvation: "Come to him, to that living stone, rejected by men but in God's sight chosen and precious" (1 Pet 2:4). Why then would Christ, who is God, give the divine title "Rock" to a mere human Apostle?

Saint Peter bore the divine name of Rock because he represented Christ on earth. This is why Saint Peter and every subsequent Pope receive the title "Vicar of

Christ." A *vicar* is someone who represents another. The term "Vice President" comes from the same Latin word. The *Vice* President stands in for the President should he be out of the country, in surgery, incapacitated, or even dead. The Vice President is not the President but he represents him. In the same way, the papal Vicar of Christ is not a divine person, but he does represent a divine Person, that is, Our Lord Jesus Christ. Peter and all successive Popes are not literally the Rock of Salvation spoken of by Old Testament writers. However, Christ appointed them to represent Him in that way, and so He built His Church upon this special office.

Why Caesarea Philippi?

To further illustrate the Roman mission of Saint Peter and His Church, Christ led His band of Apostles far north to the city of Caesarea Philippi. "Now when Jesus came into the district of Caesarea Philippi, he asked his disciples, 'Who do men say that the Son of man is?'" (Mt 16:13).

Caesarea Philippi was in the northernmost part of Palestine near the ancient city of Dan. It is important not to confuse it with the other Caesarea on the Mediterranean coast. Caesarea Philippi rests along the foothills of Mount Hermon, which is the largest mountain in the whole area, lifting up 2,814 meters above sea level. This elevation is nearly four times higher than the temple mount in Jerusalem, which is only 741 meters above sea level!

Why did Christ lead them here? Most commentators note that there was as an enormous wall of rock that was one hundred feet high and five hundred feet wide at Caesarea Philippi. These commentators suggest that Christ used this large rock as an illustration. They are correct up to this point, but most miss the significance of what was *built on top of this massive rock.* On top of this rock was a temple dedicated to the "divine" Caesar Augustus! Here in the Holy Land of Israel was an idolatrous temple erected to the emperor of the Roman Empire! This is why Christ brought the Apostles to Caesarea Philippi. It was the site in Israel that brought one closest to the heart of the emperor worship of Rome. The blasphemy of the Fourth Kingdom of Rome was erected as a pagan temple here in Caesarea Philippi. For this reason, the city was named Caesarea.

Daniel describes a terrible Fourth Kingdom that is conquered by the Son of Man by means of a stone that grows and fills the earth. In fulfillment of the Danielic prophecy, Christ then establishes a man as the Rock near the site of an idolatrous shrine to the Roman Emperor and gives to him the Keys of the Kingdom. Christ knew that the temple dedicated to Caesar at Caesarea would not be Peter's last encounter with a Roman Caesar. By leading the Apostles to Caesarea Philippi, Christ introduces them to Rome without actually going to Rome. He chooses this site in order to connect Peter's mission with the apostate counter-mission of the Roman Empire.

The Church Infiltrates Rome

The Book of Acts is like Virgil's epic poem the *Aeneid*. In the *Aeneid*, Virgil describes the journey of the Trojan warrior Aeneas to Italy where he becomes the patriarch and ancestor to the mighty Romans. It is a myth that attempts to connect the great warriors of Troy to the founding of Rome. However, the Book of Acts is not a myth. It is a historical account of the Catholic Church's beginning in Jerusalem and finding its way to Rome.

The Book of Acts begins in Jerusalem with the Ascension of Christ and the descent of the Holy Spirit on the day of Pentecost. The last chapter of the Book of Acts summarizes the journey in this way: "And so we came to Rome," and ends with the words: "And [Paul] lived there two whole years at his own expense, and welcomed all who came to him, preaching the kingdom of God and teaching about the Lord Jesus Christ quite openly and unhindered" (Acts 28:14, 30-31). This odd ending has puzzled biblical commentators. Yet there is a simple solution to this unusual ending.

The Book of Acts ends in Rome because the story's purpose has been fulfilled. The Book of Acts follows the journey of Christianity from Jerusalem to Rome, and then it unexpectedly ends. This is not an accident—the *Romeward* thrust is the guiding force of the Book of Acts.

Everyone remembers when Saul set out on the road to Damascus and experienced a vision of the risen Christ. Rabbi Saul became Saint Paul and the rest is history. But the Book of Acts records a second vision in which Christ comes and speaks directly to Paul. This second vision is the clearest proof that our Lord Jesus Christ chose Rome to be the center of His Church on earth. "The following night the Lord stood by him and said, "Take courage, for as you have testified about me at Jerusalem, so you must bear witness also at Rome" (Acts 23:11). The Book of Acts is summarized in this single verse. Christ did not say, "Go to Antioch," or "Go to Alexandria." He said, "Go to Rome." The city of Rome, then, was explicitly shown to be integral to the divine plan. It is as if Christ is saying, "I'm moving my capital from Jerusalem to Rome and I need you to play a part in it."

What about Peter? Is not Rome the Holy See of Peter? Technically speaking, the Pope is the successor of both Peter and Paul since Catholic tradition holds that both Peter and Paul laid down their lives in martyrdom in the city of Rome.[35] Pope John Paul II explains:

In this regard it is interesting to underscore the reference of tradition to the two Apostles associated in their martyrdom with this Church. The Bishop of Rome is the Successor of Peter; however, he can also be called the heir of Paul, the greatest representative of the early Church's missionary efforts and of the wealth of her charisms. The bishops of Rome have generally spoken, taught, defended Christ's truth, celebrated pontifical rites and blessed the faithful in the name of Peter and Paul, the "princes of the Apostles," the *olivae binae pietatis unicae* ("the twofold olive-branch of a singular piety"), as is sung in the hymn for their feast on June 29. The Fathers, the liturgy, and iconography often depict this association in martyrdom and glory.[36]

Peter and Paul therefore provide the united and singular witness that established Rome as the Mother and Mistress of all Christians.

We read in Acts that there were Roman Jews in attendance when the Holy Spirit was poured out upon the Apostles on the great festival of Pentecost in A.D. 33. These Roman Jews returned to Rome and brought their faith with them.

Consequently, the early assembly of Christians in Rome was primarily Jewish. Sometime around the year A.D. 42, Herod Agrippa murdered Saint James the Greater and imprisoned Saint Peter in order to appease the Jewish leadership of Jerusalem (Acts 12). Peter escaped from prison through the miraculous intervention of an angel. The narrative ends with Peter escaping to an unnamed location. "Then he departed and went to another place" (Acts 12:17). Catholic tradition affirms that Peter's departure to "another place" was in fact an anonymous reference to Peter's first visit to Rome in A.D. 42.[37] The identification of Rome as the anonymous location of Peter's whereabouts between 42 and 49 would explain several historical mysteries. First, the Book of Acts depicts Peter as being entirely absent from Jerusalem between the years A.D. 42 and 49. Second, it would explain the Jewish riots that occurred in Rome and eventually led to the Edict of Claudius in A.D. 49. Third, it would explain why Peter suddenly reappears in Jerusalem in 49. Fourth, it would explain the apparently ridiculous assertion of the ancient *Liber Pontificalis* recording the pontificate of Peter in Rome as lasting twenty-five years, from A.D. 42 till 67.

A simple reconstruction of historical events is able to harmonize all of these facts. If Peter's escape to "another place" is in fact an anonymous reference to Rome, then this would place Peter's arrival in Rome at A.D. 42. Saint Peter would have established the early community of baptized Christians in Rome. Some of these early Roman Christians would have had heard Peter preach during their pilgrimage to Jerusalem during Pentecost in A.D. 33.

When Peter arrived in A.D. 42, he would have begun his apostolic mission of evangelization, beginning first with the Roman Jews, but also with the Roman Gentiles. The role of Gentiles in the Church was a fiery topic in the early church. It was debated throughout the Church, and the official ruling had not yet been disseminated throughout the Church.

Through the conversion of Cornelius the Roman centurion, Peter had received divine instruction allowing Gentiles to receive baptism and full status in the Church. Peter would have preached that circumcision, Jewish holy days, kosher laws, and all of the ceremonial laws of Moses were null on account of the Gospel of

Christ. This was no doubt controversial for Jewish converts and would have isolated the Jewish Christians from the rest of the Hebrew community. Peter's presence in Rome hastened the growing tension between Jews who believed in Christ and Jews that rejected Christ.

Roman Controversy over "Chrestus"

This Jewish rift surrounding the message of Peter would explain one of Roman history's most unusual episodes. In A.D. 49 the Emperor Claudius expelled all Jews from the city of Rome. Not a single Jew was allowed to remain in the city. The Roman historian Suetonius provides us with the reason. Suetonius records that the Roman Jews engaged in continual riots insinuated by "Chrestus their ringleader."[38] There is no other historical record of a Roman Jew named "Chrestus." The Roman authorities knew only that some Jews united around "Chrestus" and some Jews were bitterly opposed to "Chrestus." The debate had become publicly dangerous! If Peter had been in Rome during this time, it would explain why the Jews became so riotous—not over a controversial Roman Jew named *Chrestus* but over a resurrected Jew named *Christus*. Many have suggested that the Roman authorities expelled the Jewish population of Rome because the Jews had become so embattled over the person and claims of *Christus*, that is, the Christ and King of the Jews. The name "Chrestus" is therefore a Roman mispronunciation of the title "Christus."

The Emperor Claudius did what was expedient. Claudius ordered the immediate expulsion of every known Jew, which would have included Peter, from Rome in A.D. 49. The riots in Rome disappeared, and Peter reappeared back in Jerusalem in the very same year (Acts 15:7). We read that Aquila and Priscilla were forced to leave Rome and relocate at Corinth (Acts 18:2). This decree may also explain why Paul described himself as having been "hindered" from visiting Rome even though he desired to go there (Rom 15:22).

Peter's presence in Rome would explain his disappearance from the Books of Acts during the years of A.D. 42-49. It would also account for the mysterious Jewish riots in Rome during this same time. Lastly, it justifies the ancient tradition that Peter came to Rome in A.D. 42. His return to Jerusalem in A.D. 49 is the occasion for the Apostolic council that officially determined the most controversial topic in the early Church, a topic well known to Peter: the role and regulations of the Church concerning Jewish and Gentile Christians.

The Council of Jerusalem, as it is known, is quite remarkable because it once and for all addressed the primary dispute of the early Church. Must a Gentile believer be circumcised and keep the Torah? That is, must a Gentile Christian refrain from pork, receive male circumcision, and observe Jewish holidays? This matter had already been settled by Peter's vision and events surrounding the conversion of Cornelius. It was further confirmed by the testimony of Paul and Barnabas who had evangelized a large number of Gentiles. James concurred and cited the Old Testament's prophecy that Gentiles were to share in the promise of salvation. However, James added that it would be fitting for Gentile Christians to "to abstain from pollutions of idols and from fornication and from what is strangled and from blood" (Acts 15:19-21). This final advice was accepted and ratified by the Apostles.[39] Sometime after this council, Peter went to Antioch where he awaited the revocation of the Edict of Claudius. This agrees with the testimony of Saint John Chrysostom:

This is the privilege of our city [Antioch] that it received in the beginning for its teacher the chief of the Apostles. For it was befitting that this city, which was crowned with the name of *Christian* before the rest of the world, should receive as its shepherd the prince of the Apostles. However after having had him as our teacher we did not prevent him, but surrendered him to imperial Rome.[40]

The Emperor Claudius died in A.D. 55, and his edict expelling the Jews from Rome was repealed the following year in 56. Roman Jews returned to Rome en masse. Scholars almost unanimously agree that this is the occasion for Paul's *Epistle to the Romans*.

Peter as the "Another Man" in Paul's Romans

We know from Paul's *Epistle to the Romans* that Aquila and Priscilla had already left Corinth, returned to Rome, and reopened their home as an oratory (Rom 16:5). Peter is not mentioned by name nor does Paul address any formal leader of the Roman Church. However, Paul's epistle reveals that something magnificent had occurred over the last several years. The Gentile Christian population in Rome had grown greatly under the absence of the quarrelsome Jewish debates over "Chrestus." We get the impression from Saint Paul's *Epistle to the Romans* that the Church in Rome is a flourishing community, whose "faith is proclaimed throughout the world" (Rom 1:8).

The Jewish Christians returning to Rome in A.D. 56 have returned to discover a very different kind of church in the imperial city of Rome. It seems that when the nascent Gentile Christians in Rome converged with the Jewish Christians returning from exile under the

Edict of Claudius, new problems surfaced for the church. The debate of Christ in Rome was no longer an intra-Jewish debate but a debate between Jewish followers of Christ and Gentile followers of Christ. Paul's *Epistle to the Romans* seems to address this debate with respect to two problems in particular.

The first problem was one that we might expect as the Jewish Christians returned to Rome in the years following A.D. 56. The Jewish Christians came back to their home and were presenting themselves as the old guard of Roman Christianity against the newly evangelized Gentile upstarts. In doing so they were "passing judgment on the brethren" (Rom 14:10) on matters of kosher laws (14:2; 21) and the observance of Jewish holy days (14:5-6). The returning Jewish Christians to Rome also seemed to believe that circumcision and the Mosaic law should be retained (Rom 2; 4-10), if not for all Christians, then at least for the Christians of Jewish ethnicity. The Jewish party also accused the Gentiles of following an alleged teaching of Paul that promoted immorality. Referring to this false rumor, the Apostle writes: "And not rather (as we are slandered, and as some affirm that we say) "let us do evil, that there may come good," whose damnation is just" (Rom 3:8). Paul dismisses this characterization outright and demonstrates how faith in Christ leads to the sanctification of the believer.

The Jewish party of the Church of Rome considered themselves to be first-class Christians on account of their Jewish ancestry, circumcision, and legal obedience. They viewed the Gentile members of the Church as second-class Christians who had faith, but none of the other ornaments of the Abrahamic tradition. Paul's long and steady argument, climaxing in the tenth chapter of Romans, demonstrates that the true heritage of Abraham is found in the patriarch's profound faith—not in circumcision or in the Law of Moses, which were subsequent to Abraham's faith. According to Paul, Jews and Gentiles stood on level ground because both groups were composed of sinners and both were justified through faith in Christ. They are brothers in Christ, not competitors for Christ.

The second problem in Rome had to do with the pride of the Gentile Christians. Paul imagines the Gentile Christians observing all the Jewish Christians returning to Rome and saying to one another, "What advantage has the Jew?" (Rom 2:1). The second chapter of Romans addresses the great privilege of the Jewish people in the context of the plan of salvation. In the eleventh and twelfth chapters of Romans, we find Paul's sober warning against the haughty attitude of the Gentile Christians toward the Jewish Christians. "For if God did not spare the natural branches [the Jews], neither will he spare you!" (Rom 12:21).

Apparently the Gentile Christians were flaunting their freedom in Christ and scandalizing the Jewish Christians. One might imagine a Gentile Christian inviting a Jewish Christian for dinner and serving him pork! Paul exhorts the Gentiles to respect the consciences of the Jewish Christians in his fourteenth chapter:

> Let us pursue what makes for peace and for mutual upbuilding. Do not, for the sake of food, destroy the work of God. Everything is indeed clean, but it is wrong for anyone to make others fall by what he eats; it is not right to eat meat or drink wine or do anything that makes your brother stumble. The faith that you have, keep between yourself and God (Rom 14:19-22).

As one reads the thirteenth chapter of Romans, one cannot help but see a concern in Paul's mind about the tenuous state of the Roman Church in relationship to Imperial Rome. Once already the emperor had exiled all Jews from the city on account of "Chrestus." Perhaps Paul was worried that the current emperor Nero Caesar might hear rumors that "Chrestus" was once again stirring up rebellion in the imperial city—this time not only among the Jews but also among the non-Jews. Paul therefore exhorts the Roman Christians to "be subject to the governing authorities," and to honor the Roman Caesar in things pertaining to civic duties (Rom 13:3-7).

It may seem rather odd that Paul does not mention Peter's name in his *Epistle to the Romans*. Protestant scholars are quick to use Peter's absence in the Epistle to prove Peter's absence in Rome, with an argument such as this: "If Peter had practiced his apostolic ministry in Rome, Paul would have referred to it. Since Paul did not mention Peter's apostolic ministry in Rome, it must be the case that Peter had not been in Rome."

Contrary to this claim let me affirm that Paul did in fact refer to Peter in his *Epistle to the Romans* though not by name. This should not come as a surprise to us because Paul elsewhere avoids the proper names of important people. This is the "principle of anonymity". The New Testament authors show a general reluctance to name names concerning certain subjects. The general pattern found in the New Testament is that if anything relates to the Roman Empire, do not be specific. This was a way to protect the Church from imperial persecution. Thus Rome is referred to as "Babylon" and "another place" and "the Beast". For example, in his *Epistle to the Romans,* the Apostle refers to Nero Caesar a number of times, but not once does he refer to Nero by name. Paul refers to Nero repeatedly as an "authority", "ruler", "servant of God", and even as a "minister" (Rom 13:2-6). Anyone who knows the diabolical character of Nero, may be surprised by these flattering titles, but there is no doubt that Paul speaks of the current emperor of his day—Nero Caesar.

In a similar fashion, Paul refers to Peter as the mysterious and apostolic "other man" of the Church of Rome. Paul states that "another man" has already laid the foundation of the Church of Rome. Paul further explains why he has not yet come to Rome: "I make it my ambition to preach the gospel, not where Christ has already been named, lest I build on the foundation of *another man*" (Rom 15:20-21). The implication is that Paul has no need to come to Rome because "another man" has already built the foundation of the Church in Rome. The sufficiency of this other man's Apostleship is manifest by Paul's doctrine that the Apostles are the only men capable of laying the foundation of the Church in Christ (Gal 1:11-24). Thus, Paul had no desire to establish the Church in Rome because he saw the Church of Rome as perfectly established by "another man" with Apostolic credentials.

Tradition identifies this "other man" as none other than Peter himself. This would explain the rather obscure reason given by Paul for his being "hindered very much" from coming to Rome (Rom 15:22). Paul was aware of his controversial status in the Church. If the Jews of Rome were rioting because of Peter, Paul would have driven them into hysteria! It would not have been appropriate for Paul to go to Rome. Paul's affirmation that Rome is fully established under Apostolic authority is seen in his desire merely "to pass through" Rome and "enjoy your company for a little" as he travels to Spain (Rom 15:24).[41]

The Church Fathers on Peter in Rome

We have already seen that Saint Paul received a divine call to "go to Rome." Did Peter receive the same calling to go to Rome? We have seen that Paul alluded to "another man" who had laid the foundation of the Church in Rome some time before A.D. 56. We also have the scriptural witness from the pen of Peter himself. In his first epistle, Peter sends his greetings from the Church "in Babylon" (1 Pet 5:13). Scholars are in agreement that Babylon was often used as a code word for Rome. For example, the Apocalypse of Saint John and the Sibylline Oracles (5:143, 159) both use the term "Babylon" to denote the city of Rome. The reason should be obvious. Rome was the fourth stage of the evil empire beginning with the first kingdom of Babylon. Rome was the heir of the savage political power that made war against Israel. Moreover, it would be quite ridiculous to believe that Peter had traveled to the deserts of ancient Babylon in what is now modern day Iraq. He is undoubtedly referring to the city of Rome.

Peter's use of the term "Babylon" in reference to his location seems to confirm that he had come to reside in Rome by the time he composed his first epistle, which scholars date to sometime before A.D. 64. According to a universal tradition, Peter was crucified *upside down* sometime during the persecution of Nero (A.D. 64-68).

This tradition seems to be confirmed in the Gospel of John. After Christ has risen again, He reinstates Peter with a threefold charge that mirrors Peters threefold rejection. Just as Peter denied Christ three times while warming himself by a "charcoal fire" so Christ reinstates him by a "charcoal fire"—the only two places in Scripture where "charcoal fire" is used (Jn 18:18 & 21:9).

When Christ reinstates Peter, He makes the following prophecy about the death of Peter:

> Amen, Amen, I say to thee, When thou wast younger, thou didst gird thyself and didst walk where thou wouldst. But when thou

shalt be old, thou shalt stretch forth thy
hands, and another shall gird thee and lead
thee whither thou wouldst not. And this he
said, signifying by what death he should
glorify God. And when he had said this, he
saith to him: Follow me (Jn 21:18–19).

Christ describes the *death* that Peter was to glorify God.
The reference is to crucifixion. Christ says, "When you
are old, you will stretch out your hands." Saint John
assumes that the readers of his Gospel know that Peter
was indeed crucified and the tradition bears witness that
Peter was in fact crucified in Rome.

The testimony of the Church Fathers of the first
several hundred years testify to the Roman residency of
Saint Peter. Saint Clement, likely writing before A.D.
100 documents the death of Saint Peter and Saint Paul
in Rome:

Let us set before our eyes the good
Apostles. There was Peter who by reason of
unrighteous jealousy endured not one but
many labors, and thus having borne his
testimony went to his appointed place of
glory.

By reason of jealousy and strife Paul by his
example pointed out the prize of patient
endurance. After that he had been seven
times in bonds, had been driven into exile,
had been stoned, had preached in the East
and in the West, he won the noble renown
which was the reward of his faith.[42]

Saint Ignatius of Antioch wrote a letter to the Roman
Christians about the year A.D. 108, a letter preserved to
this day. Ignatius was the bishop of the Church of

Antioch and he acknowledges that he has no authority over the Christians of Rome. Ignatius tells the Romans, "I do not, like Peter and Paul, issue commands to you." Ignatius of Antioch, writing only forty years after the death of Peter, believed that both Peter and Paul "issued commands" to the universal Church.

Writing to Pope Soter in about A.D. 178, Dionysius of Corinth wrote: "You have thus by such an admonition bound together the plantings of Peter and Paul at Rome and Corinth."[43] Here Dionysius confirms that Peter and Paul "planted" the Church at Rome, and that Pope Soter had bound Corinth by his commands. The mention of "binding" no doubt refers to Saint Peter's binding on heaven and earth, as mentioned by Christ in Matthew 16:19.

Next, in the year 190, Saint Irenaeus of Lyons recorded that Saint Matthew composed his Gospel, "While Peter and Paul were evangelizing Rome and laying the foundation of the Church." One line later, Irenaeus explains the reason for Rome's important status: "...Indicating that tradition derived from the Apostles, of the very great, very ancient, and universally known Church, founded and organized at Rome by the two most glorious Apostles Peter and Paul."[44] This is perhaps the most important second-century Patristic witness to Petrine primacy centered in Rome.

Also around the year A.D. 190, Clement of Alexandria, writing in Egypt, confirms the tradition of Peter's founding of the Church in Rome: "As Peter had preached the Word publicly at Rome, and declared the Gospel by the Spirit, many who were present requested that Mark, who had followed him for a long time and remembered his sayings, should write them out."[45] Most scholars believe that the Gospel of Mark is actually the memoirs of Peter, collected and edited by Mark after the death of Peter in Rome. This would make sense of Peter's own words, when referring to the Church as feminine he writes, "She who is at Babylon, who is likewise chosen, sends you greetings, and so does my son Mark" (1 Pet 5:13). Here again, "Babylon" is code for "Rome." Tradition holds that Saint Peter sent Saint Mark to found the Church in Egypt at Alexandria.

Tertullian, writing around the year 218, speaks of "those whom Peter baptized in the Tiber River."[46] The Tiber River is of course the waterway running along the western side of Rome. Tertullian also writes, "How happy is its church, on which Apostles poured forth all their doctrine along with their blood! Where Peter endured a passion like that of the Lord, where Paul was crowned in a death like that John [the Baptist]."[47] Tertullian here speaks of the crucifixion of Peter and the beheading of Paul in Rome. Tertullian also records for us that Saint Clement, the fourth bishop of Rome was "ordained by Peter" at Rome.[48]

Origen of Alexandria, writing around A.D. 230 records that Peter, "having finally come to Rome, was crucified head-downwards, because he had requested that he might suffer this way."[49] Also in Alexandria after the Diocletian persecution in A.D. 303, Peter the Archbishop of Alexandria, confirms that Saint Peter was crucified in Rome. "Thus Peter, the first of the Apostles, having been often apprehended, and thrown into prison, and treated with ignominy, was last of all crucified at Rome."[50] Lactantius, an advisor to the Emperor Constantine, also wrote that, "Peter and Paul preached at Rome,"[51] and we know that Constantine constructed the old Saint Peter's Basilica over the confirmed tomb of Saint Peter at the Vatican Hill outside of the city of Rome.

The Patristic references to Peter in Rome become even more common after Council of Nicaea in A.D. 325. For example, Saint Jerome refers to his duty to consult the Pope who sits on the throne of Saint Peter. In a letter to Pope Saint Damasus, Saint Jerome wrote:

"I think it my duty to consult the chair of Peter, and to turn to a Church whose faith has been praised by Paul...My words are spoken to the successor of the fisherman, to the disciple of the cross."[52]

Also in the fourth century, Saint John Chrysostom, that great defender of Catholic orthodoxy, said that Rome holds a special primacy on account of Saint Peter:

> I love Rome even for this, although indeed one has other grounds for praising it, both for its greatness, and its antiquity, and its beauty, and its population, and for its power, and its wealth, and for its successes in war. But I let all this pass, and esteem it blessed on this account, that both in Peter's lifetime he wrote to them, and loved them so, and talked with them whiles he was with us, and brought his life to a close there.[53]

Saint Gregory of Nyssa also celebrated Peter's presence in the Church of Rome: "Which was more to the interest of the Church at Rome, that it should at its commencement be presided over by some high-born and pompous senator, or by the fisherman Peter, who had none of this world's advantages to attract men to him?"[54]

While one could assemble dozens of other Patristic sources that testify to Peter's crucifixion and burial in Rome, we will close with one by Pope Saint Leo the Great who reigned from Peter's chair from A.D. 440-461:

> The whole world, dearly-beloved, does indeed take part in all holy anniversaries of Peter and Paul, and loyalty to the one Faith demands that whatever is recorded as done for all men's salvation should be everywhere

celebrated with common rejoicings. But, besides that reverence which to-day's festival has gained from all the world, it is to be honored with special and peculiar exultation in our city, that there may be a predominance of gladness on the day of their martyrdom in the place where the chief of the Apostles met their glorious end. For these are the men, through whom the light of Christ's gospel shone on thee, O Rome, and through whom thou, who wast the teacher of error, wast made the disciple of Truth.[55]

These selections demonstrate that our most ancient Christian documents testify that Peter was indeed in Rome. Moving now from these ancient witnesses, we turn to the most recent archeological evidence regarding the excavation of Saint Peter's skeleton beneath the Vatican. Science and Tradition converge with Scripture to confirm that Christ built His Catholic Church quite literally on Peter.

NOTES

[32] For examples, see Mt 10:2; Mk 3:16; Lk 6:14; Acts 1:13.

[33] For examples, see 1 Cor 1:12, 3:22, 15:5; Gal 1:18, Gal 2:9, 11, 14.

[34] The Greek Septuagint text of Daniel reads *lithos* for stone. There is no Aramaic Targum of Daniel in existence, so it is impossible to compare how the Aramaic would render "stone" in Daniel 2:34, 35, 45.

NOTES CONTINUED

[35] When speaking *ex cathedra*, the Popes declare "by the authority of our Lord Jesus Christ, of the Blessed Apostles Peter and Paul."

[36] John Paul II, *General Audience,* January 27, 1993.

[37] See Arthur Stapylton Barnes, *Christianity at Rome in the Apostolic Age* (Westport, Connecticut: Greenwood Press, 1971), pp. 2-13, where Barnes provides a lengthy argument in support of the claim found in the *Liber Ponficalis* stating that twenty-five years elapsed from Peter's first arrival in Rome to his martyrdom in Rome, i.e. A.D. 42-67.

[38] Suetonius, *Claudius*, 25.

[39] The prohibition against eating strangled meat is missing in some manuscripts, which could mean that there were only three prohibitions pertaining to basic morality: idolatry, fornication, and "blood" – perhaps a reference to bloodshed.

[40] Saint John Chrysostom, *Second Homily on the Acts.*

[41] A.S. Barnes suggests that Romans 15:10-12 might be construed as Paul communicating the following idea: "I have long desired to come to you Rome, but I have not done so, for Peter, whose special charge you are, has been absent, and I have not liked to pay even a passing visit under those circumstances, lest I should even seem to be interfering in his special work." The Epistle to the Romans then demonstrates Paul's respect for the preeminent authority of Peter's unique apostolic ministry. Arthur Stapylton Barnes, *Christianity at Rome in the Apostolic Age* (Westport, Connecticut: Greenwood Press, 1971), p. 44. A.S. Barnes has further suggested that Peter is the one who in fact prompted Paul to write this epistle to the Church in Rome. Barnes reasons that Peter himself knew that Paul was being maligned in Rome as a lawless teacher who had taught his followers

NOTES CONTINUED

to disregard Moses and "sin boldly" on account of the superabundant grace of God through Christ. Paul therefore designed his *Epistle to the Romans* as his magnum opus—a defense of his orthodoxy to the Church in Rome that would universally acquit Paul of antinomianism as the epistle disseminated to the rest of the Church.

[42] Saint Clement of Rome, *1 Clement* 5:3-5

[43] Dionysius of Corinth, *Epistle to Pope Soter,* fragment in Eusebius' Church History, II:25

[44] Saint Irenaeus of Lyons, *Against Heresies*, 3:1-2.

[45] Saint Clement of Alexandria, cited by Eusebius in *Ecclesiastical History*, 6, 14, 6.

[46] Tertullian, *On Baptism*, 4.

[47] Tertullian, *Prescription against Heretics*, 36.

[48] Tertullian, *Prescription against Heretics*, 32.

[49] Origen of Alexandria, *Third Commentary on Genesis.*

[50] Peter of Alexandria, *The Canonical Epistle,* 9.

[51] Lactantius, *The Divine Institutes*, 4, 21.

[52] Saint Jerome, *Epistle to Pope Damasus,* Epistle 15.

[53] Saint John Chrysostom, *Commentary on Romans,* Homily 32.

[54] Saint Gregory of Nyssa, *To the Church at Nicomedia,* Epistle 13.

[55] Pope Saint Leo the Great, *Sermon* 82.

6. THE TOMB OF SAINT PETER IN ROME

Holy men...took down his body secretly and put it under the terebinth tree near the Naumachia, in the place which is called the Vatican.

- Passion of Saints Peter and Paul
Fifth Century

THE CATACOMBS OF ROME provide a historical witness to the profound faith and charity of the early Roman Christians. Within the catacombs are more than 30,000 inscriptions in Greek and Latin. These inscriptions preserve the prayer and praise of those seeking to serve Christ in dark times. These specimens of pious graffiti also reveal how Roman Christians venerated their martyred confreres and prayed for the deceased.

One of the most notable examples of early Christian inscriptions is a slab from a sealed tomb belonging to a child named Asellus, who was a Christian boy who had lived, according to the inscription, five years, eight months and twenty-three days. The tomb dates to the year A.D. 313—the year that Constantine issued the Edict of Milan tolerating Christianity. The engraving holds historical significance because it depicts the two patrons of Rome—Peter and Paul. To the left of the inscription we observe an early depiction Saints *Petrus* and *Paulus*, with the *Chi Rho* monogram of Christ above the name of Peter.

This burial monument demonstrates that the Christians of Rome believed themselves to be under the special patronage of their apostolic founders, Peter and Paul.

This early burial monument is only the tip of the iceberg. Recent archeological evidence has uncovered the actual bones of Saint Peter. As mentioned previously, the exact location of Peter's grave has been preserved for the past twenty centuries under the high altar of Saint Peter's Basilica at the Vatican. Tradition states that Peter was crucified upside down sometime during the persecution of Nero (A.D. 64-68).

Saint Peter was crucified in the outdoor racetrack known as the Circus of Nero between *duas metas* ("two turning-posts") near the obelisk in the center of the circus.[56] This obelisk was later moved to its current location in the middle of Saint Peter's square. That obelisk is likely the last physical object that Peter saw before he died. The location of the obelisk can be identified in the center of the Circus of Nero overlaid with the Old and New Basilicas of Saint Peter.

After Peter was crucified near the obelisk, his dead body was buried outside the Circus of Nero on the slope of the Vatican Hill. It would have been just to the north of the Via Cornelia, a road that ran along the northern side of the Circus.

Tropaion of Saint Peter

At some time around A.D. 200, the Roman Gaius wrote to the Phrygian Proclus concerning the tomb of Saint Peter: "I can point out the trophies (*tropaia*) of the Apostles. For if you would go to the Vatican, or to the Ostian Way, you will find the trophies (*tropaia*) of those who founded this church."[57]

What are the "trophies of the Apostles" to which Gaius refers? The Greek word is *tropaion* from which we derive the English word *trophy*. The term refers to a monument, shrine, or memorial. It seems that pious Christians had built a simple monument over Peter's tomb at the Vatican Hill. The monument on the Ostian Way refers to the burial site of Paul.

The original monument built over the tomb of Saint Peter was over ten feet tall and consisted of a travertine marble tabletop that stood suspended over the gravesite. This marble tabletop was attached to a red plastered wall and two marble columns supported its outer edge. A concave niche was carved into the wall behind the tabletop, as depicted below. This monument stood directly over the buried body of Saint Peter.

Tropaion over the Tomb of Saint Peter
A.D. 147-161

When was the Tropaion constructed? Excavators have discovered that the constructor of this monument had installed a drain to carry water away from the so-called Red Wall. The drain had been made with bricks from a Roman workshop and five of them bore the same maker's stamp. They came from a brick factory in production between A.D. 147 and 161. All scholars recognize that brick stamps prove that this is the exact monument mentioned by Gaius sometime around A.D. 200.

Who built this monument? The *Liber Pontificalis* records that Pope Anacletus, the third Bishop of Rome, "built and set in order a memorial shrine (*memoriam*) to the blessed Peter where the bishops might be buried."[58] However, Anacletus would have been Pope sometime between A.D. 79-88. This date seems too early. It is likely that the name of Pope Anacletus was confused with that of Pope Anicetus, the Pope who reigned from A.D. 155-166. The papacy of Pope Anicetus corresponds with the age of the bricks dating from A.D. 147-161. This theory would explain why the *Liber Pontificalis* incorrectly states that Pope Anacletus built the Tropaion sixty years after his death.

A persecution of Christians under the Emperor Decius in A.D. 251 may have forced the removal of the remains of both Saint Peter and Saint Paul from their burial sites to the Catacombs of Saint Sebastian where they would remain safe. At a later date, when the persecution subsided, Peter's relics were brought back again to the Vatican Hill and Paul's relics returned to his original burial site on the Ostian Way.

During this time, the Red Wall supporting the *tropiaon* had cracked. Perhaps it broke when Christians dug up the remains of Saint Peter. In order to repair the Red Wall, someone built a buttress along the cracked portion of the wall. The excavators called this buttress the Graffiti Wall, so as not to confuse it with the Red

Wall and because it was covered in Christian graffiti. The Graffiti Wall prevented the Red Wall from falling over onto the monument. As we shall see, this simple construction would eventually become the most important element of the shrine.

Constantine's First Basilica

Coins have been found at Saint Peter's burial site reaching back to the first century. The dates of these coins reveal that the tomb goes back to the first centuries of Roman Christianity. The site would not receive architectural excellence until Christians could worship openly and freely. Enter Constantine the Great.

Constantine not only granted toleration to the Church in A.D. 313, but he also supplied the Roman Church with funds for construction. He initiated building projects to honor Rome's most honored martyrs and relics. Constantine decided that a great monument of imperial grandeur should be erected to honor the remains of Saint Peter. Instead of rebuilding the makeshift Tropaion of Saint Peter built up against its Red Wall, Constantine kept the ramshackle monument intact. The architects did nothing to try to restore the disproportion caused by its crude supporting buttress. It appears that the Tropaion had reached its awkward but final form. Constantine simply left the Tropaion of Saint Peter as it was, but the emperor encased the architecturally obtuse Tropaion in a house of marble. He then built a basilica around it in order to accommodate large crowds of Catholic pilgrims. The following diagram illustrates Peter's grave in relation to Constantine's old Basilica and the present day Basilica of Saint Peter.

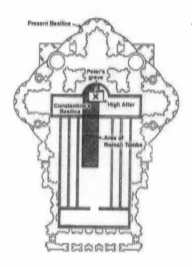

Constantine's building project required a radical modification in the natural landscape of the Vatican. Constantine had the Vatican Hill leveled and the slope below Peter's grave filled in with dirt in order to create a level grade on which to build a proper shrine. This became the original Basilica of Saint Peter—often called Old Saint Peter's Basilica. The Basilica was built before A.D. 333.

Subsequently, Saint Gregory the Great (590-604) placed an altar on top of the Constantine monument. Pope Calixtus II (1119-1124) added another altar. This crumbling Constantinian basilica stood until 1506 when Pope Julius II commissioned Donato Bramante to draw plans for the new Basilica of Saint Peter, with the further additions of the facade and the plaza. The new Basilica is the one so familiar to us today. The present altar over the tomb of Saint Peter was added by Pope Clement VIII (1592-1605). The following diagram reveals the cross section of the site and reveals the stacking of the altars on top of one another.

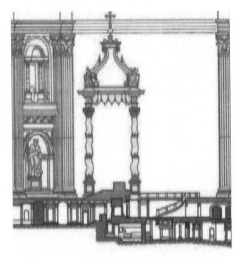

Cross section of stacked altars in Saint Peter's

The City of the Dead

Popes, pilgrims, and architects of subsequent centuries had always assumed that Peter was buried down there somewhere. However, the vault containing the grave of Saint Peter had not been accessed since the ninth century. Even then, no one was sure that the bones of Peter were really down there. All that changed in 1939 when Pope Pius XI died.

Pope Pius XI had requested that his body be buried within the grottoes under Saint Peter's Basilica in proximity to the site where it was believed that the relics of Saint Peter were reserved. Well long before he was Pope, Pius XI had been the Archbishop of Milan. During that time, the Catholics of Milan had commissioned a marble sarcophagus for their archbishop, not expecting him to be elected as Pope in 1922. When Pius XI died, the Milanese sent the marble sarcophagus to Rome for his burial.

There was a problem. The Milanese sarcophagus did not quite fit into the tomb planned for Pope Pius XI. In order to accommodate all the parties involved, Pope Pius XII decided to lower the floor. Lowering the floor revealed a long forgotten secret. Just below the floor, workers found tombs and eventually a necropolis or "city of the dead." The graves were mostly pagan. Formal archeological excavations began in 1940 and lasted until 1949. Pius XII appointed a team of five men to oversee the excavation: 1) Monsignor Ludwig Kaas, Administrator of Saint Peter's Basilica, 2) Rev. Antonio Ferrua, S.J., 3) Rev. Engelbert Kirschbaum, S.J., 4) Bruno Apollonj Ghetti, the Vatican Architect, 5) Professor Enrico Josi, Inspector of the Catacombs. Monsignor Kaas was the team's leader and the only one of the five who did not belong to the Papal Institute for Christian Archaeology. Pius XII laid down only one rule: No digging around under the altar where the bones of Saint Peter supposedly lay hidden.

Nevertheless, they secretly excavated under the floor of the Basilica's grotto toward the altar. They found a series of pagan tombs and mausoleums – large rooms that housed the cremated remains of ancient Romans. The digging continued to lead the excavators toward the area beneath the high altar of Saint Peter's.

One day, Father Kirschbaum crawled in a cramped space and shined his flashlight around only to find that yellow light reflected back at him. He beheld a golden mosaic embellished with a decorative mosaic grape vine with leaves of green. The vine framed three mosaics on the walls.

On the eastern wall, Father Kirschbaum saw the figure of a man falling from a ship and into the mouth of a giant fish. It was the story of Jonah, an image of Christ's resurrection.

> For as Jonah was three days and three nights
> in the belly of the whale, so will the Son of

Man be three days and three nights in the
heart of the earth. (Mt 12:40)

On the northern wall, Father Kirschbaum observed the
figure of a fisherman who had caught a fish, while
another fish swam away. The third mosaic on the
western wall depicted the figure of a shepherd carrying a
sheep upon his shoulders, a common motif of Christ.

Interestingly, all three of these mosaics refer to Saint
Peter. Peter was named "Simon Bar *Jona*" or "Simon
Son of *Jonah*" (Mt 16:17). Christ promised that he would
make Peter a "fisher of men" (Mt 4:18). Lastly, Christ
commissioned Peter to be a shepherd when He
exhorted him with the words: "Feed my lambs…Tend
my sheep…Feed my sheep" (Jn 21:15-17).

Excitedly, Father Kirschbaum raised his flashlight
again toward the ceiling of the tomb and focused his
eyes on the depiction in the middle of the golden
mosaic. He saw a chariot pulled by two powerful white
horses. A bearded man in a flowing cloak stood in the
chariot. The man's right arm was raised in blessing while
the left hand held a large globe, a symbol of universal
dominion. A halo surrounded the man's head and rays
of light emanated outward in the shape of a cross.

Father Kirschbaum recognized the image as a
depiction of the myth of Helios, the Greek sun god.
Helios was supposed to die every day with the setting of
the sun and rise again with the sunrise the next morning.
However, this mosaic had been adapted in such a way as
to suggest that Christ was the ascended God who had
risen like the sun, surrounded in the golden light of the
sun. The excavators had found their first Christian
tomb!

A thorough excavation of the tomb revealed that
three Christians had been buried under the floor of the
chamber. The mausoleum had originally been built to
house the cremated ashes of a pagan child. Sometime

around A.D. 250 the family of this child converted to Christianity and decorated the chamber with the Christian motifs.

The archeological team then approached Pope Pius XII and asked for permission to continue their dig and excavate under the high altar. The tomb of the golden mosaic proved that Christians had been buried in the vicinity. Perhaps they would find similar decorations if they discovered Saint Peter's tomb. Pope Pius XII required Monsignor Kaas and his four colleagues to keep complete silence. They could not speak to anyone about the excavations under the high altar until a full report could be assembled on the findings.

Did They Find Saint Peter Beneath the High Altar?

Many doubted the tradition that Saint Peter was buried under the high altar of the basilica. It seems that only Monsignor Kaas firmly believed that the bones of Peter lay below in the darkness. The other four excavators believed it to be a pious but unfounded tradition. Even if a tomb had been down there, it was assumed that Constantine had tampered with the area in such a way as to make the matter inconclusive.

The excavation team soon enough found the Red Wall. They found the Tropaion or monument built against the Red Wall – the same one that Gaius had described in 200. Father Kirschbaum scooted down and began to find bones. Pope Pius XII was summoned and he sat in a chair above as Father Kirschbaum delivered up pieces of bone to his excited colleagues. All told there were about two hundred fifty fragments of bone. Noticeably missing was the skull. This was actually a positive sign since tradition holds that the skull of Saint Peter had been hidden above the high altar at the Basilica of Saint John Lateran (along with the skull of Saint Paul). They had found human bones in the burial site that was unquestionably the grave of Saint Peter under the Tropaion. Pope Pius XII and the excavation team felt certain that they had in fact found the bones of Peter the fisherman. Oddly enough, the excavators could not find the name of "Peter" inscribed anywhere in relationship to the grave or the Tropaion.

Pope Pius XII ordered that the bones be sealed in lead boxes and secretly transported to his private apartment. The Pope's personal physician Dr. Galeazzi-Lisi and a few other medical doctors examined the bones. These doctors reported that the bones belonged to a stoutly built male who had died between the ages of sixty-five or seventy. If Saint Peter was martyred sometime between A.D. 64-68, then the bones correspond perfectly.

The bones remained secret as World War II erupted. By 1945, the excavations were coming to a close. Pope Pius XII had designated 1950 as Jubilee Year of pilgrimage. In order to kick off the Jubilee, Pope Pius XII planned to announce the findings of the excavations on Christmas Day, 1949. However, someone leaked the secret in August 1949 that the papal excavators had found the tomb and bones of Saint Peter. On August 22, 1949, the New York Times headlined an article by Camille M. Cianfarra reading: "Bones of St Peter Found under Altar Vatican Believes—Reported to be in Urn Guarded by Pontiff."

Of course, there were some who doubted that the bones belonged to Saint Peter. Pope Pius XII did indeed bring in neutral experts. In the mid-1950s, Pope Pius XII commissioned an expert anthropologist Dr. Venerando Correnti of Palmero University to study the bones found along the Red Wall. Dr. Correnti laid out all the bone fragments and began his meticulous study. There was not a complete skeleton but only pieces of bone jumbled together. It would be difficult to determine the age and sex of the person. Dr. Correnti did not seem as confident as the personal physician of the Pope who reported that the remains belonged to a stoutly built man in his late sixties.

The first thing Dr. Correnti noticed was that there were three fibulas (the thin bone of the lower leg). A human being only has two fibulas so obviously the bones revealed the remains of at least two people. Dr. Correnti subsequently noticed that there were six tibias (the thicker bone of the lower leg). Since each human being has only two tibias, it was safe to conclude that there were at least three skeletons jumbled together. Dr. Correnti then discovered that at least fifty or more of the two hundred and fifty bone fragments were *animal bones*—horses, cows, goats, and sheep!

Putting the animal bones aside, Dr. Correnti eventually concluded that there were only three human skeletons present. Two of the three had died in their fifties and were male. Since Peter was at least in his sixties when he was martyred, these two skeletons could *not* be Peter. That left the third skeleton. Dr. Correnti concluded that this third skeleton belonged to a person that had died after the age of seventy. Peter indeed!

Not quite. By measure the remains of the extent pelvis, Dr. Correnti concluded that the seventy-year-old bones belonged "almost certainly" to a woman. Dr. Correnti's conclusion was that the bone collection found in the dirt below the Red Wall was composed of bone fragments belonging to two fifty-year-old men, one seventy-year-old woman, and numerous barnyard animals. Saint Peter was not present. Or was he?

The Missing Piece of the Peter Puzzle

There is one missing piece of information that at first seems rather incidental. Monsignor Kaas, the nominal excavation supervisor, and Father Kirschbaum the Jesuit did not get along. Monsignor Kaas believed the excavators were too reckless in their techniques. Father Kirschbaum thought Monsignor Kass was unqualified and overly scrupulous. They avoided each other like the plague. By day, Father Kirschbaum and his colleagues would excavate the tombs below the floors of the basilica. By night, Monsignor Kaas would explore the site with one of the foremen by the name of Giovanni Segoni.

Several years earlier, one night in 1942, Monsignor Kaas told the foreman Giovanni Segoni to shine his flashlight into the cavity. The light revealed bones. Monsignor Kaas, in an unprofessional act of paranoia, told Segoni to remove the contents from the cavity in the Graffiti Wall. The contents amounted to bone fragments, fragile pieces of cloth, threads, and two corroded coins. These items were placed in a wooden box upon which Segoni wrote the words *ossa urna graf—* graffiti urn bones. A few days later Father Kirschbaum and his three colleagues returned to examine the man-made cavity in the Graffiti Wall and found it disappointingly empty of anything significance.

Ten years later in 1952, Pope Pius XII allowed a Greek inscription specialist from the University of Rome to examine the Christian graffiti scribbled on the Graffiti Wall. Her name was Dr. Margherita Guarducci. She examined the shallow scratches in the Graffiti Wall. It seemed to be gibberish. However, she was able to discern an inscription in the Graffiti wall that others had not noticed:

PETRUS ROGA XS IHS	*Peter, pray to XS IHS*
PRO SANCTIS	*("Christ Jesus")*
HOMINIBUS	*for the holy*
CRESTIANUS	*Christian men*
AD CORPUS TUUM	*buried near your body Peter*
SEPULTIS PETRUS	

As Dr. Guarducci re-examined the surrounding graffiti in the wall, she realized that the graffiti, like contemporary graffiti, is written in a kind of code. She noticed the recurrence of AO. This seemed to be a reference to *Alpha and Omega,* an obscure title of Christ from the Book of Revelation (Apoc 1:8; 21:6; 22:13). She also found the *chi rho* (XP) monogram denoting Christ. Stylized forms of MA referred to Maria. Stylized forms of PE referred to Peter. Dr. Guarducci also discovered that occasionally the XP was overlapped with PE to form a union with Christ and Peter. Dr. Guarducci began to wonder why this simple buttressing wall had become an object of great veneration and literally covered with Christian graffiti. Even more significantly, a broken piece of plaster was found inside the cavity of the Graffiti Wall bearing letters Greek letters: PET ENI

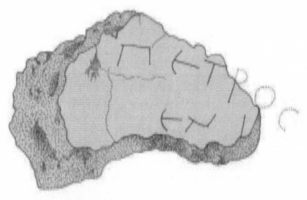

This broken fragment is interesting because the Greek word ENI means "in here." What does "PET" mean? The second half of the word has been broken off, but it has been suggested that the full word is PETROS, the Greek spelling of the name *Peter* as it appears in the New Testament.

One day, Dr. Guarducci asked Giovanni Segoni about the empty cavity in the Graffiti Wall. "Giovanni, do you remember what sorts of things were found inside that cavity?"

Segoni remembered the discovery ten years ago and answered, "Yes, I emptied it myself when old Monsignor Kaas gave the order. I can show you the things if you want."

Segoni retrieved the old wooden box. "Here, this is it."

Dr. Guarducci looked at the box marked *ossa urna graf* – "bones urn graffiti." Inside were bones, the cloth, the threads, and the coins. She wrapped the box in brown paper and stored it away.

The Mystery Revealed

It would not be for another ten years for the contents of that wooden box to be examined. In 1962, Dr. Venerando Correnti, the same anthropologist who determined that the grave bones consisted of two men in their fifties, a woman in her seventies, and several animals, turned his attention to the 135 bones in the wooden box marked *ossa urna graf.*

Dr. Correnti found the complete skeleton of a mouse and the decayed bones of one man. The mouse had likely fallen into the cavity of the Graffiti Wall and died therein. This was an act of divine providence because the mouse skeleton revealed something every important.

The bones of the mouse were bleached white whereas the bones of the man were brown and dirty. The difference in color revealed that the bones of the man had once been buried. Chemical analysis proved that the dirt adhering to the bones of the man matched the dirt from the central grave below the Tropaion. These bones had in fact at one time been buried in the earth below.

Further tests confirmed that the cloth fragments found with the bones had been once dyed purple. The accompanying threads were of solid gold and had been woven into the cloth. Dr. Correnti felt confident that these bone fragments did indeed belong to "a man of robust constitution" between the age of sixty and seventy. The bone fragments were decayed but pieces belonged to nearly every portion of the body except the feet.

Could this be Saint Peter? If so, why had he been exhumed and placed in the cavity of a shabby supporting buttress, wrapped in what seemed to be a cloth of purple and gold? And why was he buried without his feet?

Recall that tradition holds that Saint Peter was buried just outside the Circus of Nero in a common grave. A Red Wall and the Tropaion were built sometime in the second century to mark the site. Sometime after that, the Red Wall cracked and the site was repaired by adding a buttress.

In the fourth century Constantine built a house of marble around the Red Wall and the Tropaion. Either at this time or sometime before, the remains of Peter were exhumed for one of two reasons. The first explanation is as follows. The bones may have been exhumed decades before the time of Constantine in order to protect the relics in a time of persecution or foreign invasion. The other (more likely) explanation is that Constantine ordered an excavation of his own in order to satisfy his own curiosity. Either way, the bones of this man in his sixties had been removed from their original resting place beneath the Tropaion.

The purple cloth interwoven with gold thread seems to indicate that these bones were definitely placed in the buttress at the time of Constantine. At this time a cavity was carved out inside the buttressing wall, and the inside walls paneled with marble. The bones were then ceremoniously wrapped in the imperial purple of the Roman Emperor and reverently sealed in the cavity of the buttressing wall. The buttressing wall subsequently became the most venerated object of the shrine, and this accounts for its being covered in Christian graffiti. The buttress became the Graffiti Wall because it contained the precious bones of Saint Peter.

What about the missing feet? There are twenty-six bones in one human foot. This means that every human being has fifty-two feet bones. Almost all the bones of the left hand were found in the collection of bone fragments, yet not a single foot bone was found in the remains from the cavity within the Graffiti Wall.

Tradition holds that Peter was not merely crucified, but crucified upside down. We can take for granted that the brutal Romans did not waste their time carefully removing the corpses of their crucified victims. Imagine how a tired Roman centurion might remove the dead body of a man hanging upside down on a cross. A simple whack at the ankles with a sword or ax would bring the body tumbling down. Perhaps this is what happened to the body of Peter so that, when pious Christians buried the body of the Apostle outside the Circus of Nero, the feet were lost.

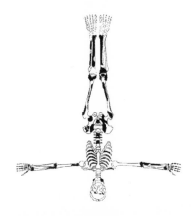

So it seems that these bone fragments are indeed mortal remains of the Fisherman. Below the high altar of Saint Peter's Basilica is Saint Peter himself. And so the words of Christ were fulfilled both spiritually and literally: *on this Rock I will build my Church*. Having now established that Peter was the Vicar of Christ, that he ministered in Rome, and that he was buried under what is now the Vatican, let us examine the first Popes that govern the Catholic Church after the death of Saint Peter.

NOTES

[56] The Emperor Caligula (d. A.D. 54), not Nero, built the "Circus of Nero" and placed in it the obelisk that currently stands in Saint Peter's Square. It is called the "Circus of Nero" because Nero popularized the arena after the city of Rome burned. Nero used the arena to stage many public spectacles. It was at this circus that Nero began the first, state-organized martyrdoms of Christians, the most notorious of which was the murdering of Christians through various means (Tacitus, *Annals*, xv. 44).

[57] Eusebius *Ecclesiastical History* 2, 25,6-7.

[58] *Liber Pontificalis* among the works of Pope Anacletus.

7. THE FIRST FIVE POPES OF ROME

Feed the flock of God which is among you, taking care of it, not by constraint, but willingly, according to God: not for filthy lucre's sake, but voluntarily: Neither as lording it over the clergy, but being made a pattern of the flock from the heart.

- Saint Peter the Apostle
1 Peter 1:2-3

THE FIRST FIVE POPES of Rome can be recalled easily by remembering that Rome is the *place*. *Place* is mnemonic device that will help you to remember the names and order of the first five Popes. Each letter in the word *place* corresponds to the first letter in each Pope's name:

Peter
Linus
Anacletus
Clement
Everistus

Many academics and scholars have called into question the existence of the early papacy. Even modernist and dissenting Catholic writers have publicly written and taught that the papacy itself cannot be found in the first generation of the Church. Their claim is that the papacy is a later invention of imperial politics.

The most common argument used by these dissenting writers is their claim that the early Church did not operate under the mono-episcopate form of polity. The term mono-episcopate refers to the arrangement by which a bishop or *episcopus* rules over a city alone. Today, the Pope appoints a single bishop who rules over a local diocese. In larger cities, there is sometimes an archbishop or bishop who is assisted by auxiliary bishops. In my own city of Dallas, we have a single bishop who is aided by two auxiliary bishops.

I have produced a detailed defense of how the mono-episcopate dates to the institution of Christ Himself in my book *The Crucified Rabbi* (Chapter Five). I have also argued in my book *The Catholic Perspective on Paul* (Chapter Eight) that Saint Paul taught and assumed the juridical structure of the mono-episcopate. It would be redundant to reproduce those arguments again in detail. Let it suffice to say that Christ appointed twelve men to rule over twelve tribes. This language assumes the Old Testament depiction of twelve judges ruling over twelve geographical jurisdictions. The command of Christ to make disciples "even to the uttermost part of the earth" (Acts 1:8) assumes that this jurisdictional model will be expanded to all nations. Christ the King rules a Kingdom—not a democracy or even an oligarchy.

Saint Peter by virtue of his name and his appointment near *Caesarea* was divinely appointed to reign from the imperial city of Rome. Peter's vocation was to transform the capital of idolatry and human pride into the capital of Christ's Divine Mercy.

Pope Saint Linus

Saint Linus is listed by all ancient documents as the direct successor of Saint Peter in Rome. Saint Irenaeus, writing about the year A.D. 180, recorded that: "The blessed Apostles, then, having founded and built up the Church, committed into the hands of Linus the office of the episcopate."[59] Saint Jerome wrote that Linus "was the first after Peter to be in charge of the Roman Church."[60] Moreover, the historian Eusebius tells us that Linus "was the first to receive the episcopate of the Church at Rome after the martyrdom of Paul and Peter."[61] The *Liberian Catalogue* and the *Liber Pontificalis* confirm the same order of succession.

Saint Linus, then, took up the reins of the Catholic Church in a very difficult and trying time. His pontificate began under Nero's cruel persecution. We may even imagine that it was Linus who presided over the burial of Saint Peter at the Vatican hill.

The *Liber Pontificalis* records an interesting detail. It describes how Saint Peter consecrated *two* bishops— Linus and Anacletus—to assist him in the governing of the Church in Rome. Peter did this, says the *Liber Pontificalis*, so as to be free to pray and preach. The same source states that Peter consecrated a third bishop, Clement, to oversee the universal needs of the Church throughout the world. The governing structure of the Church in Rome before the martyrdom of Saint Peter looked like this:

Peter
(Pope)

Linus & Anacletus
(Auxiliary Bishops in Rome)

Clement
(Papal Secretary, Bishop)

Roman Presbyters

Roman Deacons

It would be natural then that the three men trusted and directly appointed by Saint Peter (Linus, Anacletus, and Clement) would succeed Saint Peter as the chief bishops of Rome in succession. This governing structure of Saint Peter's Roman Church might also explain a statement of Saint Jerome, which reads that Clement "was the fourth bishop of Rome," but that "most of the Latins think that Clement was second after the Apostle."[62]

Linus, it would seem, was chief among these men and the most well-known. That Linus was a prominent Christian in Rome is clear from the testimony of Sacred Scripture. Saint Paul mentioned Saint Linus as being in Rome in the late 60s just before the martyrdom of Saints Peter and Paul. The Apostle wrote to Saint Timothy saying: "Make haste to come before winter. Eubulus and Pudens and Linus and Claudia and all the brethren, salute thee" (2 Tim 4:21). In this final epistle of Saint Paul before his martyrdom, the Apostle includes the names of those prominent in the Roman Church—Linus being one of them.

Tradition holds that the Pudens, the man Paul listed along with Linus, volunteered his home to Saint Peter as the first domestic church building of Rome. Pudens' father was the Roman senator Quintus Cornelius Pudens and his mother was Saint Priscilla—two of the first converts of Saint Peter. The family allowed Saint Peter to use Quintus' senatorial chair or *cathedra* for liturgical ceremonies. Hence, Pudens' home was the first cathedral of Rome. Here Pudens and his daughters Pudentia and Praxedes hosted the Apostles.

This home became known as the *ecclesia pudentiana*—the Pudentian Church. It is revered as the oldest Catholic church in Rome. From the time of Saint Peter until the conversion of Constantine in A.D. 313, this location was the home and headquarters of the Popes.

Eventually, the wooden altar of Saint Peter was removed from the Church of Saint Pudentiana and placed within the high altar at the Basilica of Saint John Lateran in Rome. In order to honor the Pudentian Church, a plank from the wooden altar was enshrined in the altar of Saint Pudentiana. This gesture symbolized that Peter's altar was originally at this location. Centuries later, when Cardinal Wiseman was titular cardinal of Saint Pudentiana he had the plank examined and found that the wood was identical with that of the wooden altar preserved at the Lateran Church. These historical and archaeological details demonstrate that Linus and Pudens were the most important Christian leaders in Rome at the time.

There are only two things that we know about Pope Saint Linus for sure. First, there is an immemorial tradition that Pope Linus decreed that all Christian women should veil their heads during the liturgy of the Church. Saint Paul, who mentions Linus in 2 Timothy 4:21 also confirms this ancient Christian tradition:

> Now I praise you, brethren, that in all things you are mindful of me and keep my ordinances as I have delivered them to you. But I would have you know that the head of every man is Christ: and the head of the woman is the man: and the head of Christ is God. Every man praying or prophesying with his head covered disgraceth his head. But every woman praying or prophesying with her head not covered disgraceth her head: for it is all one as if she were shaven. For if a woman be not covered, let her be shorn. But if it be a shame to a woman to be shorn or made bald, let her cover her head. The man indeed ought not to cover his head: because he is the image and glory of

> God. But the woman is the glory of the
> man. For the man is not of the woman: but
> the woman of the man. For the man was not
> created for the woman: but the woman for
> the man. Therefore ought the woman to
> have a power over her head, because of the
> angels (1 Corinthians 11:2–10).

No doubt, Pope Saint Linus was merely reiterating what
Saint Paul had taught before him about chapel veils.

The second thing we know about Pope Saint Linus
was that he was a martyr like Peter before him. He is
commemorated in the Roman Canon of the Mass as a
martyr of the primitive Church along with Pope Saint
Anacletus (Cletus) and Pope Saint Clement:

> Having communion with and venerating the
> memory, first, of the glorious Mary, ever-
> virgin Mother of our God and Lord Jesus
> Christ, likewise of Thy blessed Apostles and
> Martyrs: Peter and Paul, Andrew, James,
> John, Thomas, James, Philip, Bartholomew,
> Matthew, Simon, and Thaddeus, *Linus,*
> *Cletus, Clement,* Sixtus, Cornelius, Cyprian,
> Lawrence, Chrysogonus, John and Paul,
> Cosmas and Damian, and of all Thy saints,
> for the sake of whose merits and prayers do
> Thou grant that in all things we may be
> defended by the help of Thy protection.
> Through the same Christ our Lord.

The *Roman Martyrology* marks martyrdom of Pope Saint
Linus as having occurred on September 23rd:

> At Rome, Saint Linus, Pope and martyr,
> who governed the Roman Church next after
> the blessed Apostle Peter. He was crowned

with martyrdom and was buried on the Vatican Hill beside the same Apostle.

A sarcophagus discovered in Saint Peter's Basilica in 1615 inscribed with the letters *LINVS* was once believed to be Linus's tomb. However, some archeologists doubt whether the tomb is that of Linus, since the inscription might merely be the last five letters of a longer Roman name such as Marcel*linus* or Aqui*linus*. Nevertheless, it is perfectly reasonable to hold that a body buried next to Saint Peter with the inscription *LINVS* is in fact the historical Pope Saint Linus.

Pope Saint Anacletus

Pope Saint Anacletus or Cletus was the third Pope and Bishop of Rome. The name *Cletus* in Greek means "one who has been called," and the variation *Anacletus* means "one who has been called back."

There is much confusion about Saint Anacletus. The *Liber Pontificalis* states that Anacletus and Cletus are two different Popes of this time.[63] However, Saint Irenaeus, the historian Eusebius, and Saint Augustine report that Saint Anacletus and Saint Cletus are one and the same person. This position agrees with the Congregation for Rites decision in 1961 that the feast of Saint Cletus on April 26 is also the feast of Saint Anacletus—the two names referring to one and the same Pope.

Saint Anacletus is known for having ordained twenty-five priests for the city of Rome. This multiplication of priests indicates that the Catholic Church in Rome had already spread over the city before the close of the first century. The bishop alone could not serve the pastoral needs of the city. Tradition holds that Saint Anacletus is buried alongside Saint Peter and Saint Linus at the Vatican hill.

Pope Saint Clement

Pope Saint Clement I is of particular interest to us since his long epistle is among the oldest Christian documents not included in the canon of Sacred Scripture. Before examining this epistle, let us examine the facts of his life. Tertullian tells us that Saint Clement was consecrated bishop by Saint Peter himself.[64] As discussed above under the entry for Saint Linus, the *Liber Pontificalis* records that Peter consecrated Linus and Anacletus to assist him in the governing of the Church in Rome and that Peter appointed Clement as bishop to oversee the universal needs of the Church throughout the world. Since these three bishops, Linus, Anacletus, and Clement, operated with episcopal authority in Rome during and after the life of Saint Peter, there may have been confusion as to their proper order. Our earliest witnesses place these Popes in their right order as detailed above.

Tradition of the universal Church identifies Pope Clement I with the Clement mentioned by Saint Paul: "And I entreat thee also, my sincere companion, help those women who have labored with me in the gospel, with Clement and the rest of my fellow laborers, whose names are in the book of life" (Phil 4:3). There was once an attempt to identify Pope Clement with Titus Flavius Clemens who was consul to the Emperor Domitian. This theory has long since been abandoned. The *Shepherd of Hermas,* a popular apocryphal Christian book of the second century explains that Saint Clement was responsible in Rome for communicating with other churches in cities throughout the empire. This detail reaffirms the account given in the *Liber Pontificalis,* which identifies Clement as overseeing the universal needs of the Church throughout the world.

Saint Clement's epistle is commonly called *First Clement* in order to distinguish it from *Second Clement*—a work ascribed to Saint Clement but now considered spurious. *First Clement* is notable in that its author asserts apostolic influence over the Christians of Corinth. Saint Clement first praises the Corinthian Christians but then refers to their current struggles with "emulation and envy, strife and sedition, persecution and disorder, war and captivity."[65]

Clement immediately focuses on Saints Peter and Paul as pillars and exemplars of Christian charity and duty. He writes:

> But not to dwell upon ancient examples, let us come to the most recent spiritual heroes. Let us take the noble examples furnished in our own generation. Through envy and jealousy, the greatest and most righteous pillars have been persecuted and put to death. Let us set before our eyes the illustrious Apostles. Peter, through unrighteous envy, endured not one or two, but numerous labours; and when he had at length suffered martyrdom, departed to the place of glory due to him. Owing to envy, Paul also obtained the reward of patient endurance, after being seven times thrown into captivity, compelled to flee, and stoned. After preaching both in the east and west, he gained the illustrious reputation due to his faith, having taught righteousness to the whole world, and come to the extreme limit of the west, and suffered martyrdom under the prefects. Thus was he removed from the world, and went into the holy place, having proved himself a striking example of patience.[66]

Saint Clement's words reveal that the Church of Rome already had the greatest respect for her martyred pillars

Peter and Paul. After listing other martyrs, Clement again focuses on the sins of the Corinthian Church and urges them to repentance and peace.

The epistle of Saint Clement is especially noteworthy in that he refers to bishops {*episcopoi*} and presbyters or priests {*presbyteroi*} ruling the Church, and to the deacons {*diakonoi*} who serve them.[67] Saint Clement, then, is one of the earliest extra-biblical witnesses to Holy Orders, apostolic succession, and the threefold office.

Most Protestant scholars object to this conclusion by observing that Saint Clement seems to use the word for *bishop* and *presbyter* interchangeably—something also done by Saint Peter and Saint Paul. The Protestant argument seeks to undermine the Catholic claim that bishops are distinct from presbyters. By asserting this interpretation, Protestants seek to deny the Catholic teaching of apostolic succession, that is, that the sacrament of Holy Orders comes to us through the unbroken line of bishops. Most Protestants deny the need for apostolic succession and favor the egalitarian arrangement of a congregation served by an appointed minister with lay elders and/or deacons.

In both volumes previous to this book, *The Crucified Rabbi* and *The Catholic Perspective on Paul*, I described at length how the threefold office is assumed and taught by Saint Peter, Saint Paul, and Saint Luke in the *Acts of the Apostles*. The short answer is that the threefold office looks like the following during the time of the Apostles:

Apostle

Bishops/Presbyters
(terms interchangeable)

Deacons

After the deaths of the Apostles (from A.D. 65 till 100), the threefold office of Holy Orders modifies to look like this

Bishop

Presbyters
(term now distinct from Bishop)

Deacons

The office of Apostle has ceased, so the successors of the Apostles employ the term *bishop* as distinct from *presbyter.* This is natural since the Greek word for *bishop* is *episcopos,* which translates to English as *overseer.* A bishop oversees his diocese. It was perfectly natural for Christians to elevate this term to the highest office of the Church.

Protestants deny this progression and seek to keep bishops equal to presbyters. However, Saint Clement explicitly teaches that the ministry at Rome and at Corinth was threefold with a monarchical bishop ruling over priests and deacons:

> These things therefore being manifest to us, and since we look into the depths of the divine knowledge, it behooves us to do all things in their proper order, which the Lord has commanded us to perform at stated times. [Christ] has enjoined sacrifices {*prosphora*} and liturgies {*leitourgias*} to be performed, and that not thoughtlessly or irregularly, but at the appointed times and hours. Where and by whom He desires these things to be done, He Himself has fixed by His own supreme will, in order that all

things being piously done according to His good pleasure, may be acceptable unto Him.

Those, therefore, who present their offerings at the appointed times, are accepted and blessed; for inasmuch as they follow the laws of the Lord, they sin not. For His [Christ's] own peculiar liturgies {*leitourgiai*} are assigned to the high priest {*archierei*}, and their own proper place is prescribed to the priests {*hiereusin*}, and their own special diaconal ministries {*diakoniai*} devolve on the Levites {*Leuites*}. The layman is bound by the laws that pertain to laymen.

Let every one of you, brethren, give thanks to God in his own order, living in all good conscience, with becoming gravity, and not going beyond the rule of the ministry prescribed to him.[68]

Here Saint Clement exhorts the lay people to honor the offices and ministry of the bishops, priests, and deacons. Clement compares the Old Testament liturgy to that of the New Testament liturgy. He notes that Christ desires sacrifices *(prosphora)* and liturgy *(leitourgias)*. In the Old Testament, the temple in Jerusalem was served by the high priest, the priests, and the Levites. Yet, Clement presumes that the same is true for the Catholic Christian. According to Clement, the sacrifices and liturgy are still celebrated by the high priest, priests, and Levites. However, here he refers to the bishop, the presbyters, and the deacons. This is also why deacons have been called "Levites" from the earliest days of the Catholic Church. The meaning is clear here in *1 Clement* since shortly after Clement cites the Septuagint version of Isaiah 60:17. "I will appoint their bishops in righteousness, and their deacons in faith." Moreover, Saint Clement explicitly relates the ministry of the "Levites" as "*diaconal* ministries." In conclusion, Saint Clement not only affirms the threefold office of bishop, priest, and deacon in Rome and Corinth, he also describes the three offices in relation to the sacerdotal arrangement of the Old Testament.

We know from tradition that Saint Clement was banished from Rome by the Emperor Trajan to serve in the stone quarries of Chersonesos, a colony located on the southwest part of Crimea on the shore of the Black Sea. When Clement arrived at the quarry, he observed that the prisoners suffered from thirst. He knelt down in prayer and asked Christ to provide water. Upon finishing his prayer, Clement saw a lamb on a nearby hill. Taking a pick from the quarry, Clement dug in the earth where the lamb had stood. Immediately, a stream of cool, clear water bubbled up from the ground. Many pagans, both freemen and prisoners were converted by this miracle and received holy baptism. The large number of conversions provoked the authorities to have Saint Clement tied to an anchor and then cast into the Black Sea in A.D. 98.[69]

Pope Saint Evaristus

The exile of Saint Clement from Rome left the Church of Rome in need of a new shepherd. Pope Saint Evaristus succeeded Clement as the fifth Bishop of Rome, having reigned from about A.D. 99 to 107.[70] His name in Greek means "well pleasing." According to the *Liber Pontificalis*, he was "born in Greece of a Jewish father named Judah, originally from the city of Bethlehem." Saint John, the last of the living Apostle, died either just before or during his pontificate. His pontificate was the first in which the personal authority of the Apostles was absent. This makes Saint Evaristus the first post-apostolic Pope of the Catholic Church.

Pope Saint Evaristus persevered under the persecution of Domitian, which is reckoned by Catholics as the Second Roman Persecution. He divided among the priests the titles of the city of Rome. Titles were approved and ratified places of worship apart from the liturgy of the Pope. The Latin word *titulus* as a term for a Roman parish is interesting. It probably derives from the Old Latin (and Vulgate) version of the Holy Bible, in which it is said that Jacob erected a *title* or altar to the Lord:

> And trembling, he said: How terrible is this place? This is no other but the house of God, and the gate of heaven. And Jacob arising in the morning, took the stone which he had laid under his head, and set it up for a title {*titulum*}, pouring oil upon the top of it (Gen 28:17-18).

According to the Roman way of seeing things, each validly erected altar in the city was a *titulis* erected by their patriarch—the Bishop of Rome. Hence, to have valid worship and communion with the Pope, one had to worship and receive the sacraments from a properly appointed *titulus*. As we read in *1 Clement* above, Pope Saint Clement had already established the custom of proper places of worship: "Where and by whom He desires these things to be done, He Himself has fixed by His own supreme will, in order that all things being piously done according to His good pleasure, may be acceptable unto Him."

Saint Ignatius of Antioch, a contemporary of Saint Evaristus, orders the same:

Let that Eucharist be held valid which is
offered by the bishop or by the one to
whom the bishop has committed this
charge. Wherever the bishop appears, there
let the people be; as wherever Jesus Christ is,
there is the Catholic Church.[71]

Both in Antioch and Rome, the bishops were
dealing with a new problem—the church was growing
quickly. The faithful could not attend the Eucharist of
the bishop. Rather, delegates were appointed by the
bishop for the celebration of the Holy Sacrifice. In the
writings of Saint Ignatius we find that the faithful
should attend the Eucharist of the bishop or the
Eucharist offered "by one to whom the bishop has
committed this charge." It comes to no surprise that
during the same exact decade, the Bishop of Rome,
Saint Evaristus, has appointed priests to the seven titular
churches of Rome. This appointment of priests and
titular churches in the city reveals that Christianity in
Rome was now spread throughout the population of
Rome. We also learn that Pope Saint Evaristus
appointed seven deacons to assist him in ministering to
the city. It would seem that these seven deacons served
the seven titular churches of Rome. The *Liber* also
records that he promoted six priests, two deacons and
five bishops, destined for various churches. Evaristus
received the crown of martyrdom in his ardent love for
Christ. He was buried near the body of Blessed Peter in
the Vatican, on October 25. His feast day is October 26.
The throne of Saint Peter remained vacant for nineteen
days until his successor, Pope Saint Alexander I was
raised to the dignity of Bishop of Rome and Vicar of
Christ.

NOTES

[59] Saint Irenaeus, *Adversus Haereses* 3, 3, 3.

[60] Saint Jerome, *Chronicon* 14.

[61] Eusebius, *Church History 3, 2*.

[62] Saint Jerome, *Illustrious Men* 15.

[63] The *Liber Pontificalis* numbers Saint Cletus as the third Pope after Saint Linus and then Saint Anacletus as the fifth Pope after Saint Clement. It seems that this confusion was due to a confusion of two names for one person: Cletus and Anacletus.

[64] Tertullian, *Prescription Against Heretics*, 32.

[65] *1 Clement* 3.

[66] *1 Clement* 5.

[67] *1 Clement* 43.

[68] *1 Clement* 40-41.

[69] Today, the Inkerman Monastery of Saint Clement marks the cave where the relics of Saint Clement were found. A local tradition states that an annual ebbing of the Black Sea reveals the place of his relics, which had been miraculously preserved in a divinely built reliquary. The relics were later enshrined in a grotto nearby where Christians would visit on the anniversary of Saint Clement's martyrdom. The remains included the bones of Saint Clement alongside the infamous anchor.

In about A.D. 868, Saint Cyril reverently transferred the relics of Saint Clement, the fourth successor Saint Peter, back to the city of Rome. The relics of Saint Clement were deposited in the most suitable church: the Basilica of Saint Clement in Rome where they remain to this day.

[70] Alternatively, Eusebius records that Evaristus died in the twelfth year of the reign of the Roman Emperor

NOTES CONTINUED

Trajan (A.D. 110), after holding the office of Bishop of Rome for eight years. *Ecclesiastical History* 4, 1.

[71] Saint Ignatius of Antioch, *Epistle to the Smyrnaeans* 8:1, in about A.D. 110.

8. ROME DESTROYS JERUSALEM

And when he drew near, seeing the city, he wept over it, saying: If thou also hadst known, and that in this thy day, the things that are to thy peace; but now they are hidden from thy eyes. For the days shall come upon thee, and thy enemies shall cast a trench about thee, and compass thee round, and straiten thee on every side, And beat thee flat to the ground, and thy children who are in thee: and they shall not leave in thee a stone upon a stone: because thou hast not known the time of thy visitation.

- Our Lord Jesus Christ
St Luke 19:41-44

THE MARK OF THE BEAST is a concept that has fascinated Christians and non-Christians alike. Various "end-times experts" have speculated about the Mark of the Beast and suggestions have been made as to what it might be: the bar code found on every single item in the grocery store, credit cards, fiat money, tattoos on the forehead and hand, or microchips implanted in the face and hand. Anyone with a deep understanding of history and the symbols of antiquity would know that these opinions are not only unlikely, but may miss the theological intent of the Sacred Scriptures. As discussed in the previous book *The Crucified Rabbi*, this is yet another reason why knowledge of the Old Testament is essential to understanding Scripture and Catholicism. The "mark" on the forehead hearkens back to Ezekiel's prophecy that the people of

God will be marked on the forehead with the ancient Hebrew letter "tau" which conforms to our letter "T." This is a prophecy that the faithful in the New Testament will be signed with the cross (signified by the letter T) on the head, as happens during baptism and confirmation.

> And the Lord said to him: Go through the midst of the city, through the midst of Jerusalem: and mark *Tau* upon the foreheads of the men that sigh, and mourn for all the abominations that are committed in the midst thereof (Ezek 9:4).

The mark of the beast, then, is counterfeit sacrament of the beast that draws people away from the true Christ.

Moreover, the mark of the beast refers back to bestial imagery of the Book of Daniel, as discussed in the first chapter of this book. Daniel foresaw the coming of the fourth Kingdom of Rome as: "a fourth beast, terrible and dreadful and exceedingly strong; and it had great iron teeth; it devoured and broke in pieces, and stamped the residue with its feet. It was different from all the beasts that were before it; and it had ten horns" (Dan 7:7). This dreadful beast with ten horns shows up again in the Book of Apocalypse. It may come as a big shock to many readers that the Book of the Apocalypse is not entirely about future events, but mostly about *past* events. When Saint John wrote the Book of the Apocalypse in the first century, he explained that the events contained in the book were concerned with things that were about to take place soon. The first line of the Book of Revelation (the most neglected verse of the entire book) reads: "The revelation of Jesus Christ, which God gave him to show to his servants what must soon take place." The events of the Book of the Apocalypse are not perceived as necessarily occurring thousands of years from the time of Saint John, but as things just around the corner.

The theological system that holds that the Book of the Apocalypse describes past events is called *preterism* as distinct from *futurism*, which holds that all the events in the Book of the Apocalypse await an entirely futuristic fulfillment. The Catholic Church does not support the "full preterist" or "strict preterist" view holding that all prophetic events described in the Scriptures are past events. The Catholic Church still believes in the coming of a future Antichrist, the second coming of Christ, the final judgment, the general resurrection of the body, and the life everlasting. The apocalyptic events of the past foreshadow the future events of the final tribulation and apocalypse at the end of time.

The mark of the beast is a perfect example to demonstrate how the Book of the Apocalypse is primarily concerned with the struggle of the newly budding Christian Church with the corrupt Jewish leadership of Jerusalem on one side, and the Roman Empire on the other side. Read how the Book of the Apocalypse describes the Mark of the Beast:

> No one can buy or sell unless he has the mark, that is, the name of the beast or the number of its name. This calls for wisdom: let him who has understanding reckon the number of the beast, for it is a human number; its number is six hundred and sixty-six (Apoc 13:17-18).

The Mark of the Beast "calls for wisdom," is a "human number," and it numbers "666." Most Scripture scholars make the preterist conclusion that Saint John is referring to the archenemy of the early Christians, the man who put to death Saint Peter and Saint Paul in

Rome: Nero Caesar. The Beast is Rome and the human leader of this Beast is the Caesar.

In antiquity, each alphabetic letter had a numeric quantity. If you add up the letters of the name *Nero Caesar* in the Hebrew language, the sum total is 666. Very early in the history of the Book of the Apocalypse, a textual variant appeared in some manuscripts of the Book of the Apocalypse that enumerated the Beast as 616 and not 666. Why the discrepancy? It seems that early copyists of the book modified the number so that the meaning wouldn't be lost to non-Hebrew readers. The name Nero Caesar in the Greek language adds up to 616, and so the scribal copyists tweaked the number so that Greek readers would perceive the hidden meaning of the text. Given this textual variant and its somewhat coincidental sum as the numeral value of *Nero Caesar* in Greek, it seems obvious that the number code is a reference to Nero.

There are other subtle hints pointing to Nero, as well. Revelation describes the Beast as having seven heads.

> This calls for a mind with wisdom: the seven heads are seven mountains on which the woman is seated. They are also seven kings, five of whom have fallen, one is, the other has not yet come, and when he comes he must remain only a little while (Apoc 17:9-10).

Again, the reader is called to have a "mind with wisdom" in order to understanding the meaning. "The seven heads are seven mountains." Pliny the Elder describes Rome as *complexa septem montes* or "nestled on seven hills."[72] Rome is known classically as the city of seven hills. This Beast is clearly the city of Rome.

The reader is also told that the seven heads are the seven "kings" of Rome. These are the seven Caesars of the rise and fall of the Julio-Claudian dynasty of imperial Rome: (1) Julius Caesar, (2) Augustus, (3) Tiberius, (4) Caligula, (5) Claudius, (6) Nero, and (7) Galba.[73] *Five have fallen* refers to the emperors from (1) Julius through (5) Claudius. These five emperors had reigned and died before the reign of Nero Caesar. *One is* – Nero Caesar who mercilessly persecuted Peter, Paul, and the Christian faithful of the empire. *The other has not come; and when he comes, he must remain a little while.* This is the seventh emperor Galba who reigned for the brief span of about seven months (8 June 68 to 15 January 69). We see that Saint John has described the list of the first seven Caesars perfectly. The Antichrist figure of the Book of Revelation ("the one who is" or the sixth emperor) is Nero Caesar.

If there is any doubt that Nero is the Satanic Antichrist of the Roman Beast it should be noted that the Book of Revelation states that the Beast blasphemed and "made war against the saints" for "forty-two months." Nero Caesar's great persecution of the Christians lasted *exactly forty-two months* from November A.D. 64 till June A.D. 68. Within this forty-two month period, hundreds of Christians received the crown of martyrdom, including the Apostles Saint Peter and Saint Paul. An understanding of Roman and Church history reveals that Nero Caesar is the human villain of the Book of Revelation.

The Catholic tradition of identifying Nero as the primordial foreshadowing of the future Antichrist is well documented in the early Church. Nero committed suicide in June of A.D. 68. The unusual death of Nero led to rumors that he had not truly died or that being a sorcerer himself, he would rise again from the dead. Soon after, false Nero imposters began to appear claiming to be Nero resurrected. The legend that Nero had returned to rule is known as the *Nero Redivivus* legend. Suetonius mentions imperial edicts forged in the name of the deceased Nero, which promised his imminent return to avenge himself on his enemies.[74] Nero appears again in the early Jewish and Christian apocryphal books *Ascension of Isaiah* and the *Sibylline Oracles*. As late as the fifth century, Saint Augustine of Hippo wrote of the *Nero Redivivus* legend.[75] The confusion about the "return of Nero" is best understood through the Catholic lens of typology. Nero will "return" not literally, but the future Antichrist will fulfill Nero's perverse lifestyle and tyrannical rule against the saints of Christ. The future Antichrist will be all that Nero was, and more.

Rome and the Structure of the Apocalypse

If Rome is the great and terrible Beast described by Daniel, and Nero Caesar is the historical personage associated with the fierce actions of the apocalyptic Antichrist, the Book of Revelation becomes much easier to understand in the context of history. The dragon of Revelation is Satan, the serpentine demon who seeks to destroy Christ and his followers. The terrible Beast is the Fourth Beast described by Daniel, the Roman Empire that issued the death sentence against Jesus Christ. The sixth king is the sixth emperor of the Roman Empire whose name adds up to 666 and who persecuted the Christians for forty-two months—Nero Caesar who foreshadows the future political Antichrist. The woman who gives birth to the Messiah represents Israel but chiefly the most blessed Israelite virgin and mother, the Blessed Virgin Mary. The New Jerusalem from above is the Church, for she is described as the Bride of the Lamb, the Lamb being Christ Himself.

There are two dominant symbolic images that remain to be identified in the Book of Revelation.

Chapter thirteen of the Apocalypse describes two different beasts: 1) the beast arising from sea, and 2) the beast arising from the land. The sea is a symbol of the "peoples and multitudes and nations and tongues" (Apoc 17:15). The Sea Beast is the Beast ruling the Gentile nations – the Roman Empire as we have seen before. This beast resembles the dragon and receives a head wound—a reference to the *protoevangelion* in Genesis 3:15, when God promised that a descendent of Eve would boot the head of the serpent.

The second beast arises from "the land." Some translations read "the earth" but the context of the Book of Revelation reveals that "the land" is a certain place. The book of Revelation uses the expression "the inhabitants the the land" twelve times to refer to the inhabitants of Israel. The land of Palestine was promised to Abraham, received after the death of Moses, and conquered by King David. The phrase "those who live in the land" refers to the *Holy Land* and the Old Testament frequently employs this phrase to refer to God's judgment against the idolatrous Israelites living in "the land."[76]

The beast arising out of "the land" is thus a beast arising out of the Holy Land of Israel. Those who worship this beast are "the inhabitants of the land," again a common prophetic motif denoting idolatrous Israel. The Land Beast had "two horns like a lamb and it spoke like a dragon" (Apoc 13:11). In other words, this beast looks and sounds good, but it is truly evil. It is the apostate High priesthood and Levitical system of sacrifice that does not recognize the sacrifice of Christ.

It may seem rather shocking to some readers that the Book of Revelation depicts the High Priest and the sacrificial system he represented as an apostate beast fostering worship of the Roman Empire. However, we should remember that when faced with the choice between Caesar and Christ, the chief priests and leaders of the Jewish people shouted: "We have no king but Caesar!" (Jn 19:15). In this moment, the chief priests of Israel changed their allegiance from the God of Israel to the Caesar of Rome. They bowed down to the Roman Beast of the Gentiles and in turn became the Beast of the Holy Land.

The Land Beast who represents the violent, apostate version of Judaism is able to work miracles through its union with the diabolic Sea Beast of Rome. The Book of Acts depicts the enemies of the Apostles as Jewish magicians (cf. Acts 8:9-24) and as ones working in concert with Roman officials (cf. Acts 13:6-11). The Land Beast also seeks to force Christians to "worship the Sea Beast" on pain of death. The Book of Acts reveals that the persecution of the early Church was almost uniquely a Jewish persecution of the faithful in concert with Roman officials.[77] Just as with the trial and murder of Christ, the apostate Jewish leadership planned their persecution in league with Roman officers. Paul himself suffered because of "the plots of the Jews" (Acts 20:19) and described this as "wild beasts" (1 Cor 15:32).[78]

The Book of the Apocalypse is a cosmic battle. It is a battle for the truth. The Church of Jesus Christ goes toe-to-toe with two fearsome enemies who have entered into an unholy alliance: Rome and Jerusalem. In brief, the Book of Revelation is an apocalyptic vision foretelling that the Church of Jesus Christ will overcome these two beasts and the demonic dragon behind their plots. It is the story of how the Church overcomes the Roman Empire and becomes the Roman Catholic Church. It is also the story of how the Church overcomes apostate Jerusalem and becomes the New Jerusalem. In both instances, the Church overcomes evil through suffering.

The Jewish-Roman War

So what did happen to Jerusalem and Rome? Jerusalem fell in a day. It took centuries for Rome to fall. Judaea became a Roman province in A.D. 6. At this time Rome began to oversee of the appointment of the High Priest. Matters became worse when the emperor Caligula declared himself to be a god and decreed in A.D. 39 that his image be worshiped throughout the Empire.

The Jewish-Roman war began A.D. 66 in Caesarea. Apparently a few members of the community sacrificed birds in front of the local Caesarean synagogue.[79] The Roman garrison turned a blind eye to the matter, further infuriating the Jewish community. At this time, the High Priest had been offering prayers and sacrifices for the well-being of Nero Caesar. The priests ceased the prayers for the emperor and his empire in order to show their disgust. Moreover, the son of the High Priest, Eliezar ben Hanania led a successful attack against the Roman garrison stationed in Jerusalem. The Roman legate of Syria, Cestius Gallus, brought in reinforcements to restore Roman order over Jerusalem, but these troops were devastated by the Jewish rebels at the Battle of Beth Horon. The Jews were victorious, at least for the moment.

When news reached Rome, Emperor Nero Caesar appointed Vespasian as general in the place of Gallus and ordered him to crush the rebellion in Judea. Vespasian marched first against northern Palestine and had squashed the Jewish rebellion by A.D. 68. For the most part, the Romans watched the Jews slaughter one another over disagreements concerning the leadership of the revolt. Shortly after this Nero Caesar committed suicide, and the Roman Empire plunged into civil war.

The year 69 is frequently referred to as the "Year of the Four Emperors". The suicide of Nero racked the Roman Empire and left a vacuum of power. Galba was immediately recognized as emperor and welcomed into the city at the head of his legions. Galba is the seventh horn of the Sea Beast that "must remain a little while" (Apoc 17:10). His rule marked the end of the Julio-Claudian dynasty. Galba was murdered by the Praetorian Guard in the middle of the Forum. That same day, the Senate recognized Otho as the Roman Emperor. After three months, Otho committed suicide rather than be humiliated by the usurper Vitellius. On the evening of Otho's suicide, the Senate recognized Vitellius as the Roman Emperor.

Meanwhile in the East, the general Vespasian had gathered popular attention for his successful march against the Jewish revolt. He had been acclaimed as the true Roman Emperor and he sought to confirm this claim. He attacked the city of Rome. Tacitus describes what Rome was like in these days:

> The whole city presented a frightful caricature of its normal self: fighting and casualties at one point, baths and restaurants at another, here the spilling of blood and the litter of dead bodies, close by prostitutes and their like – all the vice associated with a life of idleness and pleasure, all the dreadful deeds typical of a pitiless sack. These were so intimately linked that an observer would have thought Rome in the grip of a simultaneous orgy of violence and dissipation.[80]

Vespasian's men captured the Emperor Vitellius in the imperial palace and murdered him. In capturing Rome, they burned down the most important religious site in Rome, the Temple of the Capitoline Jupiter. The Temple of Jupiter, king of the gods, had been destroyed, but a new king had taken his place in Rome: Emperor Vespasian, the fourth emperor of the year A.D 70.

The Destruction of Jerusalem

The Emperor Vespasian arrived in Rome in A.D. 70. He had left his son Titus Flavius in Judaea in order to ensure that the Jewish Revolt was finished once and for all. Although Vespasian tamed Judaea, Jerusalem had not yet been captured by the Roman troops. This last task had been left to Titus.

The Roman armies built a permanent camp outside the city. They had dug a trench around the circumference of the walls of Jerusalem and built a second wall of their own around the city. The Romans captured any Jew fleeing the city and crucified them along the outer wall within sight of the inhabitants of Jerusalem. Tens of thousands of crucified bodies circled the city of Jerusalem—a terrible reminder of the expedient crucifixion of a Jew named Jesus who had claimed to be the Messiah exactly forty years previous.

Titus had four legions stationed around the city. Three legions were stationed along the western side and the fourth legion was encamped on the Mount of Olives. Titus restricted all food and water supplies into the city. At one point, Titus had the famous Jewish historian Flavius Josephus negotiate terms for surrender with his fellow Jews.

Tacitus records that there were six hundred thousand inhabitants defending Jerusalem from inside. Men, women, and children engaged in armed resistance.

By May of A.D. 70, Titus was breaking through the walls of Jerusalem while he catapulted stones weighing one talent into the city. These stones are likely the "plague of hailstones weighing one talent" described in the book of Revelation (Apoc 16:21). Titus set his sight on the strategic Fortress of Antonia just north of the

Temple. The Fortress of Antonia was the second highest point in the city, and occupying it would enable the Romans to directly attack the Temple Mount. However, Jewish attacks prevented him from constructing the siege towers necessary for capturing the Fortress of Antonia.

Unable to build siege towers or scale the walls of the Fortress, the Romans successfully attacked sleeping guards and captured the Fortress of Antonia. Titus sought to capture the Temple Mount from this position. At some point, a Roman soldier threw a burning torch into one of the Temple's windows, igniting a raging fire. As the Temple burned, the Romans looted it and massacred the defenders. Titus passed through the veil and entered the Holy of Holies out of curiosity. He reported that the room was completely empty. He was amazed to find nothing: not an idol, not an artifact, not even a scroll. This confirms the historical fact that the Ark of the Covenant and the two attendant statues of the cherubim were lost when the First Temple was destroyed by the Babylonians in 586 B.C.

Before long the flames spread so that the Temple could not be spared. It seems that Titus did not want to destroy the Temple. Rather he had likely desired to transform the Temple into a shrine to his father the Roman Emperor and possibly to the Roman pantheon. According to Josephus (who tends to portray Titus in the best light) the Roman soldiers had grown to despise the Jewish people and so purposely set fire to the Temple, contrary to the explicit orders of Titus.

Whatever the case, the fire in the Temple could not be quenched, and so Titus, having visited the Holy of Holies, watched it burn. The destruction of the Temple on *Tisha B'Av* (August 29 or 30), crushed the morale of the Jews, as it signaled the beginning of the end. Some of the remaining Jews made a heroic last stand in the upper part of Jerusalem; however, the Romans successfully captured the city by September 7, 70. Josephus wrote:

> This was the end which Jerusalem came to by the madness of those that were for innovations; a city otherwise of great magnificence, and of mighty fame among all mankind.[81]

The Little Apocalypse of Christ

The destruction of Jerusalem is not a coincidence of history. The Fathers of the Church generally understood the horrific events culminating up to the year of A.D. 70 as the apocalyptic "end of the age." This was not the end of time, but rather the end of the Jewish age centered on Jerusalem with its priesthood and sacrifices.

The late 60s had seen the great fire of Rome, the first imperial persecution of Christians, the martyrdoms of all the Apostles (except John), including Peter and Paul in Rome under Nero, the Jewish revolt, the suicide of Nero, the end of the Julio-Claudian imperial dynasty followed by the year of the four emperors, and the final destruction of the Temple and Jerusalem. It was no doubt a time of great tribulation.

Christ foretold this time of tribulation in what is known as the "little apocalypse" recorded in Matthew chapter 24, Mark 13, and Luke 21:

> Jesus left the temple and was going away, when his disciples came to point out to him the buildings of the temple. But he answered them, "You see all these, do you not? Truly, I say to you, there will not be left here one stone upon another that will not be thrown down."

As he sat on the Mount of Olives, the disciples came to him privately, saying, "Tell us, when will this be, and what will be the sign of your coming and of the close of the age?"

And Jesus answered them, "Take heed that no one leads you astray. For many will come in my name, saying, 'I am the Christ,' and they will lead many astray. And you will hear of wars and rumors of wars; see that you are not alarmed; for this must take place, but the end is not yet. For nation will rise against nation, and kingdom against kingdom, and there will be famines and earthquakes in various places: all this is but the beginning of the birth-pangs.

"Then they will deliver you up to tribulation, and put you to death; and you will be hated by all nations for my name's sake. And then many will fall away, and betray one another, and hate one another. And many false prophets will arise and lead many astray. And because wickedness is multiplied, most men's love will grow cold. But he who endures to the end will be saved. And this gospel of the kingdom will be preached throughout the whole world, as a testimony to all nations; and then the end will come.

"So when you see the desolating sacrilege spoken of by the prophet Daniel, standing in the holy place (let the reader understand), then let those who are in Judea flee to the mountains; let him who is on the housetop not go down to take what is in his house;

and let him who is in the field not turn back
to take his mantle.

And alas for those who are with child and
for those who give suck in those days! Pray
that your flight may not be in winter or on a
Sabbath. For then there will be great
tribulation, such as has not been from the
beginning of the world until now, no, and
never will be. And if those days had not
been shortened, no human being would be
saved; but for the sake of the elect those
days will be shortened. Then if any one says
to you, 'Lo, here is the Christ!' or 'There he
is!' do not believe it. For false Christs and
false prophets will arise and show great signs
and wonders, so as to lead astray, if possible,
even the elect. Lo, I have told you
beforehand. So, if they say to you, 'Lo, he is
in the wilderness,' do not go out; if they say,
'Lo, he is in the inner rooms,' do not believe
it. For as the lightning comes from the east
and shines as far as the west, so will be the
coming of the Son of man. Wherever the
body is, there the eagles will be gathered
together.

"Immediately after the tribulation of those
days the sun will be darkened, and the moon
will not give its light, and the stars will fall
from heaven, and the powers of the heavens
will be shaken; then will appear the sign of
the Son of man in heaven, and then all the
tribes of the earth will mourn, and they will
see the Son of man coming on the clouds of
heaven with power and great glory; and he
will send out his angels with a loud trumpet

call, and they will gather his elect from the four winds, from one end of heaven to the other.

From the fig tree learn its lesson: as soon as its branch becomes tender and puts forth its leaves, you know that summer is near. So also, when you see all these things, you know that he is near, at the very gates. Truly, I say to you, this generation will not pass away till all these things take place" (Mt 24:1-34).

The church historian Eusebius records that the Christians who lived in Jerusalem in the 60s observed that the "little apocalypse" prophesied by Christ was coming to pass and so they fled Jerusalem during the withdrawal of Cestius Gallus in A.D. 66. Most of the elements of the "little apocalypse" came to pass.

The Temple was certainly torn down (24:2). There were certainly wars in both Rome and Judea (24:6-7). The Apostles were literally persecuted and killed (24:9). Josephus records the coming of many false messiahs (24:5, 23-24). The uncircumcised Titus standing in the Holy of Holies is the "desolating sacrilege spoken of by the prophet Daniel, standing in the holy place" (24:15). The reference to "eagles" surrounding the city refers to the military standards born by every Roman legion (24:28), which bore the unmistakable image of an eagle.

The greatest indicator that the little apocalypse is a prophecy of the Roman siege and destruction of Jerusalem is that Christ gives the date for these events: "Truly, I say to you, this generation will not pass away till all these things take place" (Mt 24:34). In the Bible, a generation is forty years. Christ uttered these words in A.D. 30. The Temple was destroyed in A.D. 70. The end of the Jewish age was accomplished through the fury of the Romans. The new age of the Church would usher in a transformation of these Romans in an unimagined way—the Roman Empire would eventually recognize Christ as the true King of Kings and Lord of Lords. Soon a Roman Emperor would bear the banner of Christ.

NOTES

[72] Pliny the Elder, *Historia naturalis,* 3, 9.

[73] Some have objected that Augustus, not Julius Caesar, was the first true emperor. However, in the first century, Julius was counted as the first emperor. Suetonius begins his *Lives of the Twelve Caesars* with Julius as the first emperor as does Dio Cassius in his *Roman History.* In his *Antiquities of the Jews*, the Jewish historian Flavius Josephus identifies Julius as the first (xixi.11), Augustus and Tiberius as the second and third (xviii.ii.2), and Caligula as the fourth (xviii.vi.10). Book 5 of *Sibylline Oracles* identifies Julius as "the first king," and 4 Esdras 12:15 identifies Augustus as "the second."

[74] Suetonius, *Life of Nero,* 57.

[75] Saint Augustine of Hippo, *City of God* 20, 19, 3.

[76] For examples of this terminology, see Jer 1:14; 10:18; Ezek 7:7; 36:17; Hos 4:1-3; Joel 1:2, 4; 2:1; Zeph 1:18.

[77] For examples, see Acts 4:1-3, 15-18; 5:17-18, 27-33, 40; 6:8-15; 7:51-60; 9:23, 29; 13:45-50; 14:2-5; 17:5-8, 13; 18:17; 20:3; 22:22-23; 23:12, 20-21; 24:27; 26:21; 28:17-29; cf. 1 Thess 2:14-16.

[78] The authors of the New Testament are not trying to foster a primitive form of anti-Semitism. They were Jews themselves. Rather, they saw perceived that the High Priests, the priests, and the leaders of the

NOTES CONTINUED

synagogues had turned away from God and joined forces with the evil empire of Rome.

[79] Josephus, *War of the Jews,* 2, 14, 5.

[80] Tacitus, *The Histories,* 3, 83; trans Kenneth Wellesley (New York: Penguin Books, 1975) p. 198.

[81] Josephus, *Wars of the Jews.* 7, 1, 1.

9. CONSTANTINE AS CAESAR RENDERED UNTO GOD

As in the time of Moses himself and of the ancient God-beloved race of the Hebrews, "he cast Pharaoh's chariots and host into the sea." In the same way, Maxentius also with his soldiers and bodyguards "went down into the depths like a stone," when he fled before the power of God which was with Constantine.

- Eusebius of Caesarea[82]

IMPERIAL PERSECUTIONS BEGAN in A.D. 64 in the aftermath of the Great Fire of Rome. The details are unclear, but tradition states that Nero intentionally had Rome set on fire. The historian Tacitus records that Nero accused the Christians of the crime and used the event as pretense to violently persecute the Church. Saint Peter and Saint Paul were martyred at this time. The subsequent persecutions escalated in the final and most severe persecution under Diocletian and Galerius. Saint Sebastian, Saint Cyprian, and Saint Agnes were martyrs of the tenth persecution.

The Catacombs

On account of persecutions, the Church in Rome was forced underground, literally. Catholic Christians received the Jewish belief that the dead would be resurrected. The Church's firm belief in the resurrection required them to reject the pagan practice of cremation. Instead, Roman Christians buried their dead in simple graves or in underground vaults. As these catacombs began to be filled with Christian martyrs, they became a sacred place where liturgical memorials were held in order to commemorate the anniversaries of the martyrs. The importance of the catacombs is evident in that the Church in Rome created an office of "grave digger" that was important enough to be reckoned as belonging to the clergy—that of *fossor* or "digger."[83] These men were charged with digging the catacombs and burying the dead, particularly the martyrs, with solemnity and care. These *fossors* were not merely ditch diggers, they were engineers. The catacombs expand below the surface of the earth in an area extending to about six hundred acres or nearly one square mile (2.4 km^2)! These chambers lie 20-65 feet (7-19 meters) below the ground. Tunnels and narrow stairwells give access to the manmade caves. Some catacombs are several stories deep. Burial chambers contain niches carved into the walls where the dead were laid.

Roman Persecution of the Church

By the end of the third century, the Church had grown accustomed to martyrdom. The third century theologian Tertullian wrote: "The blood of the martyrs is the seed of the Christians."[84] In other words, the Church grows through the constant testimony of the martyrs who perfectly conform their lives *and their deaths* to the pattern of Christ. These early Christians remained faithful to Christ in the face of impending torture, rape, and death. The fidelity of these early martyrs is forever enshrined in the Roman Canon of the Holy Sacrifice of the Mass. In the prayer *Communicantes*, we hear pronounced the names of twelve Roman martyrs who laid down their lives as a witness to their love for Christ.

Linus, Cletus, Clement, Sixtus, Cornelius,
Cyprian, Lawrence, Chrysogonus, John and Paul,
Cosmas and Damian and all the saints. May their
merits and prayers grant us your constant help and
protection. Through Christ our Lord. Amen.

The first five names were martyred Popes of the Roman
Church. Cyprian was a North African bishop who
suffered martyrdom in the seventh Roman persecution
under Emperor Valerian. Lawrence was a Roman
deacon who received martyrdom at the time of Valerian
as well. The last five names denote lay martyrs of the
Roman Church. Cosmas and Damian were twin
brothers martyred in the last persecution under
Diocletian and Galerius. This collection of popes,
clergy, and laymen reveals that the Roman persecutions
struck at every level in the Church.

Saint Augustine counted ten Roman persecutions of
the Catholic Church beginning at the time of Saint Peter
and ending at the time of Constantine the Great.[85]

1. Persecution under Nero (c. 64-68)
    Martyrdoms of Peter and Paul.
2. Persecution under Domitian (c. 81-96)
3. Persecution under Trajan (112-117)
    Christianity is outlawed but Christians are
    not sought out.
4. Persecution under Marcus Aurelius (c. 161-
    180). Martyrdom of Polycarp
5. Persecution under Septimus Severus (202-
    210). Martyrdom of Perpetua
6. Persecution under Decius (250-251)
    Christians are actively sought out by
    requiring public sacrifice. Could buy
    certificates (libelli) instead of sacrificing.

Martyrdoms of bishops of Rome, Jerusalem, and Antioch.

7. Persecution under Valerian (257-59)
   Martyrdoms of Cyprian of Carthage and Pope Sixtus II of Rome.
8. Persecution under Maximinus the Thracian (235-38)
9. Persecution under Aurelian (c. 270–275)
10. Severe persecution under Diocletian and Galerius (303-324)

For those of us living in free nations, it is difficult to understand how Christians could be steadily persecuted for almost three centuries. We know from early documents and records that early Christians were frequently accused of cannibalism, incest, and atheism. Outsiders did not know that Christians referred to the Eucharist when they spoke of eating the "body and blood" of Christ. Moreover, spouses referred to one another as "brother" and "sister" since both shared a common father. Outsiders did not know that their common father was the "Heavenly Father." To complicate matters, Christians did not pray to the gods. They were atheists only in the sense that they rejected the Roman gods and secretly worshipped the one true God. The early Christian apologists wrote extensively on these matters and quickly dismissed the rumors circulated about Catholic Christians.

There was one matter, however, that could not be clarified so as to satisfy the pagan Romans. Romans were expected to honor the emperor with divine worship. This was accomplished either through words of homage or through ritual offerings, usually the offering of incense to an image of the emperor. Baptized Christians owed all their worship to Christ and could by no means share this allegiance with the Caesar of Rome. Not even a small pinch of incense could be offered to an image of Caesar without denying every tenant of the Christian faith. Christians stood firm, and they paid with their blood.

By the end of the third century, Christians found that they were being persecuted not only by the sword, but also with the pen. In 270 the Neo-Platonist philosopher Porphyry aimed his intellectual powers against Christianity. In that year, Porphyry began his fifteen-volume work *Against the Christians* in which he sought to disprove the Christian faith from a philosophical point of view. Porphyry claimed that "the evangelists were the inventors, not the historians of those things they record about Jesus."[86]

In 298 a riot occurred in Antioch. Pagan priests accused Christians of disrupting the pagan sacrifices of the city. Just as the fire of Rome had previously provoked Nero to initiate the first Roman persecution, so this event provoked the last and bloodiest of Rome's persecutions against the Christians.

At this time, the Eastern Roman Empire was ruled by the Augustus (senior emperor) Diocletian and the Caesar (junior emperor) Galerius. In 300 Galerius issued an imperial edict requiring all Roman soldiers to offer sacrifice. This command compromised the multitude of Christian soldiers serving in the Roman army. Any solder that refused to offer sacrifice received the death penalty. According to tradition, Saint George, the patron of soldiers, received martyrdom on account of this policy.

On February 23, 303, Galerius published edicts that ordered the destruction of Christian property, the arrest of all clergy, and the burning of Sacred Scripture. When the senior emperor Diocletian fell ill, Galerius took advantage of the moment and immediately extended his persecution to the citizens of the empire. All were ordered to offer sacrifice to the gods on pain of death.

The situation was different in the Western Roman Empire. The senior Emperor Maxentius and the junior emperor Constantius followed a lax policy toward the Christians. In the East, junior emperor Galerius soon replaced Diocletian as the senior emperor, and Galerius redoubled his efforts to stamp out Christianity in the Eastern Roman Empire. As the years wore on, Galerius suffered from a terrible bowel disease and feared that the God of the Christians had punished him for his incessant persecution of the Church. Galerius issued an edict of toleration toward the Christians on April 30, 311, but he died a few days later on May 5, 311.

The death of Galerius in 311 left a vacuum of power in the Roman Empire. Prior to this, Diocletian had placed the Roman Empire under a tetrarchy of four co-reigning emperors. A senior and a junior emperor governed the Western half of the empire; and a senior and a junior emperor governed the Eastern half of the empire. The senior emperors received the important title of "Augustus" while the junior emperors received the lesser title of "Caesar". Diocletian stipulated that when the senior emperor retired or died, the junior emperor would take his place and choose a new junior emperor or Caesar. This system "solved" the crisis of imperial succession. In fact, the tetrarchy did not solve the problem of succession, but only complicated the matter. It would soon be resolved by Constantine the Great.

The Roman Empire Recognizes Christ

Authors have hailed Constantine as either a providential benefactor of the Church or a nefarious opportunist who cursed civilization with the shackles of Christendom for over a millennium. Constantine's victory over his political enemy Maxentius at the Milvian Bridge stands out as one of the most important junctures of human history. The miraculous events surrounding Constantine's victory and his subsequent toleration, even endorsement, of Christianity set the stage for the Catholic Church's influence throughout Europe.

His full name was Flavius Valerius Aurelius Constantinus. He was the son of the Western Roman Emperor Constantius Chlorus and his first wife Helena. Within the hierarchy of the Roman tetrarchy, Constantine's father Constantius Chlorus reigned as a Caesar or junior emperor, and his territory included northern Europe, Spain, and Britain.

In 305, the two senior ruling Roman *Augusti* stepped down, thus elevating the two junior *Caesares* to become the Empire's two *Augusti*. This meant that Constantine's father became the senior emperor or Augustus of the West. However, one year later on July 25, Augustus Constantius Chlorus died at York, England, and his legions responded by hailing his son Constantine as the senior Roman Augustus of the West. This was complicated because the Eastern Augustus Galerius recognized Constantine merely as a junior emperor (Caesar) and not as a senior emperor (Augustus). Instead, the Eastern Augustus Galerius promoted Severus to the title of Western Augustus.

The death of Galerius led to chaos and the political confusion came to a head in 312 when Constantine marched on Rome to challenge the appointed senior emperor Maxentius in battle. This battle would determine who would be recognized as the true Augustus of the West. All expected Maxentius to remain within the walls of Rome and wage a defensive battle. However, Maxentius consulted soothsayers who reported favorable omens that he would conquer Constantine. Overly confident, Maxentius chose to make his stand against Constantine at the Milvian

Bridge, a stone bridge that carries the Flaminian Road over the Tiber River into Rome.

Meanwhile on the evening of October 27, 312, Constantine received a vision. He saw a cross in the heavens and heard the Latin words: *In hoc signum vinces* ("In this sign you will conquer"). The Christian author Lactantius reports that Constantine was commanded in a dream to "delineate the heavenly sign on the shields of his soldiers."[87] He obeyed and marked the shields with a sign "denoting Christ. This likely refers to the *Chi Rho* monogram that appears as the Greek letter *chi* ("x") interposed with the Greek letter *rho* ("p"). The *chi* and the *rho* are the first two letters in the Greek word for Christ: XRISTOS pronounced *Christos*.

We possess two accounts of the "Battle of the Milvian Bridge" by the church historian Eusebius. In his earlier *Ecclesiastical History*, Eusebius relates how God assisted Constantine but is silent concerning any details about visions and staurograms emblazed on the shields of Constantine's legions. In his later *Life of Constantine*, Eusebius relates the story as Constantine himself told it to him.

According to Constantine, he looked up into the sun and saw a cross of light suspended over the sun along with the words: *In this sign you will conquer*. These words are best known in their Latin translation: *In hoc signo vinces*. Constantine was puzzled by this miraculous sign and wondered at the meaning of it. That same evening, Constantine testified that he received a dream in which the Lord Jesus Christ charged him to use the revealed sign against his enemies. The imperial standards bore this sign, and the *Chi Rho* monogram continued to serve as Constantine's imperial standard for the rest of his life. Constantine credited his victory over Maxentius at the Milvian Bridge to the power of Christ. Secular historians debate the reliability of these accounts. Against the revisionist argument is the historical fact that Constantine began minting coins with the Christian *Chi Rho* staurogram as early as 315. The existence of these coins testify to the historical reality of Constantine's conversion to Christ. It may not have been a thorough conversion, but Constantine was already publicly displaying his faith just three years after the Battle of the Milvian Bridge.

Constantine the Great or Not-So-Great?

We know for certain that Constantine's mother was a Christian. The Catholic Church still invokes her as Saint Helena. While the Eastern Orthodox Church also invokes Constantine as *Saint* Constantine, the Roman Catholic Church has a rather less optimistic appreciation for Constantine and has never granted him the honor of sainthood. The uneasiness of the Catholic Church in this regard is due to the fact that Constantine did not formally identify himself as "Christian" until he was at least forty years of age.[88] Moreover, he received baptism just prior to his death.

For better or for worse, his reluctance to embrace Christ publicly in baptism was likely based on his deference to the Roman political agenda. He was baptized only before his imminent death. However, if we judge Constantine by his deeds, he seems to have been a great advocate of Christianity. He inaugurated construction on Rome's holy sites by building the original Old Saint Peter's Basilica, the Basilica of Saint Paul's Outside the Walls, and the Basilica of Christ the Savior or Saint John Lateran. He not only exempted the Church from taxes, but even subsidized it with state funds. With the help of his mother he also commissioned the Church of the Holy Sepulcher in Jerusalem to house the tomb of Christ. It seems that Daniel's prophecy was becoming realized. Through the sacrifice of Christ and the suffering of the Church, the majesty of Rome had been transformed into an instrument of the Gospel. The Roman Empire became a tool in the hand of the Church.

Constantine wisely perceived that the emerging Catholic Faith would glue together his fragile Empire. However, he knew that the adhesive nature of the Faith would only hold if that faith remained one. Two heresies threatened the unity of the Church: Donatism and Arianism. Donatism was a rigorist movement that held that the sacraments administered by a lapsed cleric were invalid and that the Catholic Church in union with the Bishop of Rome was lax and corrupt. The Arian heresy taught that God the Son was not fully divine like God the Father but that the Son was merely the first and highest creature of the Father.

Constantine did not sit back and let these heretical movements jeopardize the unity of the Church or the unity of the Empire. In 316, Constantine settled a North African dispute concerning the Donatists. He ruled in favor of the Catholics. More significantly, in 325 Constantine convened the Council of Nicaea, remembered as the first Ecumenical or Universal Council of the Catholic Church. This council stood down the Arians and issued the Nicene Creed. Although modified in 381, the Nicene Creed is still recited every Sunday in every Catholic cathedral and parish in the world.

Five years later in 330, Constantine did the unthinkable. He moved the capital of the Roman Empire *away* from Rome to the rebuilt city of Byzantium. He renamed this city *Roma Nova* or "New Rome" and established it with a Senate and imperial hierarchy corresponding to the glories of Rome. It was a

Christian city, and Constantine consecrated the new capital with the true cross of Christ found in Jerusalem by his mother Helena along other sacred relics. Constantine erected the extravagant Church of the Holy Apostles over the site of the temple of Venus. Statues of the Greek and Roman gods were modified to conform to angels, saints, or Christian virtues. After his death, this city of Byzantium that Constantine had renamed *Nova Roma* became known simply as Constantinople or "Constantine's City".

Only seven years after Constantine the Great had founded his Eastern capital at Byzantium he fell sick on Easter day in 337. Seeking healing, Constantine left Constantinople for the hot springs near the city of Helenopolis, a place Constantine named after his mother Helena. It was here that Constantine realized that he was dying, and so he attempted to return to Constantinople and ready himself for death. He never made it. Coming as far as Nicomedia, Constantine begged to be baptized and received the sacrament from the bishop of Nicomedia, a certain Eusebius. He had delayed baptism, claiming that he hoped to be baptized in the Jordan River like Christ. Constantine died on May 22, 337. He was sixty-five years of age. His body was transferred to Constantinople and interred in the Church of the Holy Apostles. There he was hailed as "Equal to the Apostles."

As stated above, the Catholic Church never canonized Constantine as a saint. Even granting Constantine's role in the Ecumenical Council of Nicaea, the Roman Church was not ready to canonize a man who was baptized on his deathbed. However, Constantine's legacy loomed large in the history of the Catholic Church. To be sure, Constantine himself was *not* the fulfillment of Daniel's prophecy. Constantine merely inherited the blessings of the Catholic Church laboring under the heavy hand of Roman persecution.

Christ did not intend for the Emperor of Rome to supercede the Bishop of Rome. It was the supernatural office of Saint Peter, not the temporal office of Constantine, that would endure over the centuries to come.

Quite interestingly, Constantine complicated the Roman legacy of the Catholic Church by creating Constantinople as the eastern imperial capital. Constantinople, as the so-called "New Rome," struggled with her Western sister Old Rome for prestige and influence. Christian emperors of Constantinople began to act like spiritual heads over their realm. Historians refer to this error as *caesaropapism*—the combination of the offices of *Caesar* and *Papa*. It is the belief that Caesars or Emperors have spiritual and supernatural jurisdiction over their subjects. Put more simply, it is the belief that the Emperor is a Pope.

Before too long, the eastern emperors of Constantinople sought their independence from true Rome. This independence was manifested as the great schism between East and West—between the Roman Catholic Church and the Eastern Orthodox Church. By entering into schism with Rome, which is the one and only divinely appointed capital of Christianity, the Eastern Orthodox perpetuated this error of *caesaropapism*. Although Constantine established Catholicism as the official religion of the Roman Empire, he also prepared the Church for schism by introducing the theoretically confusing idea of a *New Rome* in Constantinople. However, a biblical understanding of Daniel's prophecy reveals that the claims of the Eastern Orthodox are completely unfounded. The Church of Rome was, is now, and will be forever the center from which Christ manifests His redemption and kingdom.

The crucifixion of Christ on a Roman cross had already inaugurated the Kingdom of God. God desires all men to be saved and He chose that His Son would die and rise again during that fullness of time in A.D. 33. The vicarious ministry of Peter in Rome laid the groundwork by which the prophecy of Daniel would come to pass:

> And the kingdom and the dominion and the greatness of the kingdoms under the whole heaven shall be given to the people of the saints of the Most High; their kingdom shall be an everlasting kingdom, and all dominions shall serve and obey them (Dan 7:26-27).

Under the complicated reign of Constantine the heathen kingdoms under heaven were at last "given to the people of the saints of the Most High." If Daniel is inspired by God (and he is), then the true Church of Jesus Christ on earth *must be Roman*. This fact compelled me to recognize the Roman Catholic Church as the true Church instituted by Our Lord Jesus Christ. Daniel's prophecy about the Fourth Kingdom and the Son of Man must be true. Moreover, history confirms it. However, imperial Rome did not last forever. The Roman Empire expired, but the Roman Church lived on.

NOTES

[82] Eusebius of Caesarea, *Ecclesiastical History* 9, 9, 5The scriptural reference employed here by Eusebius is from Exodus 15:5.

[83] Saint Jerome, Epistle 49.

[84] Tertullian, *Apologeticum* 1.

[85] Augustine, *City of God* 18.52.

[86] From Macarius, *Apocriticus* II:12.

[87] Lactantius, *De Mort. Pers.* 44, 5.

[88] Peter Brown, *The Rise of Christendom* 2nd edition (Oxford: Blackwell Publishing, 2003), 61.

10. City of Man or City of God?

I was so confounded by the havoc wrought in the West and above all by the sack of Rome that, as the common saying has it, I forgot even my own name. Long did I remain silent, knowing that it was a time to weep.

- Saint Jerome[89]

THE RISE AND DECLINE of Rome have been used as political paradigms for every great nation. Powerful nations cannot help but compare themselves to the stature of ancient Rome. The Byzantine Empire never repudiated its status as the "Roman Empire" long after the fall of Rome in the West. Even after the fall of Constantinople, Moscow claimed to be the "Third Rome." When we recall the rise of the medieval Holy Roman Empire, it's worth noting that it was neither holy nor Roman in the strict sense of the terms. Even King Henry VIII and his prelates justified his headship over the Church of England by citing the obvious authority of Constantine over the Council of Nicaea in 325 (and everyone knew that Constantine was first crowned on English soil at York). Lord Byron identified George Washington as "Cincinnatus of the West," a reference to the celebrated agrarian general of pre-imperial Rome. Even Napoleon styled himself as a Roman emperor.

The Fall of Rome

In his *Decline and Fall of Rome*, Edward Gibbon described Christianity as the poison that killed off the great and noble Roman Empire. His interpretation of the fall of Rome has been widely accepted until recently. The eminent church historian Jaroslav Pelikan has shown that the fall of Rome was not an isolated instance of political failure, but was actually the "social triumph of the ancient church."[90] The decline of Rome during the dispensation of Christian ascendancy is perhaps the greatest social upheaval in the history of mankind.

The great city of Rome no longer governs a vast pagan *empire* stretching from Britain to Africa to the Middle East, but the Pope of Rome today does in fact govern the world's largest demographically identified society: the Catholic Church, stretching out to every inhabited continent on the planet. The fulfillment of Daniel's prophecy was not fulfilled politically; it was fulfilled by the reign of a Rabbi crucified under Pontius Pilate.

The traditional date for the fall of Rome is 476. However, just as Rome was not built in a day, neither did it exactly fall in a single day. It is agreed that Rome had over-expanded herself beyond her borders. To make matters worse, by the year 376 Gothic tribes began to flee westerly into the Roman Empire so as to avoid the savage, nomadic people known as the Huns. Two years later, the Goths severely weakened the Roman Empire's eastern army at the Battle of Hadrianopolis, which occurred in what is today modern Turkey. As early as 382, Saint Jerome forewarned a Christian woman named Marcella of the coming fall of pagan Rome and urged her to flee from Rome.[91]

By 401, the Goths began to descend into northern Italy under the leadership of their chieftain Alaric. In 406 the barbarian tribes known as the Vandals, the Sueves, and the Alans crossed the Rhine and settled into

Gaul. These tribes began to extend through Europe so that by 429 the Vandals had crossed the Straits of Gibraltar and entered into northern Africa.

The chieftain Alaric and his Gothic hordes captured and sacked Rome in August of 410. When the siege began, the Roman inhabitants were forced to reduce their rations progressively until their stores were exhausted. As the Romans died, their bodies remained unburied and eventually illness seized the population. According to tradition, a rich lady pitied the starving and plagued Romans and so opened the gates to the Gothic enemy.

The Goths burned the city's magnificent structures and most of the slaves defected, not surprisingly, to the side of the Goths, leaving Rome devastated and undefended. Alaric allowed his followers to seize the city's wealth, and he instructed them to plunder even the domestic homes of the Romans. There is one great and miraculous exception to the greed and cruelty of Alaric. Alaric held regard for the wooden Basilica of Saint Peter, or "Old Saint Peter's," perched along the Vatican Hill, which had been commissioned by Constantine in about 324 and finished by his son Constantius in about 354. Alaric decreed that the shrine was to be honored as an asylum, although Gibbon relates "the holy precincts of the Vatican and the apostolic churches could receive a very small proportion of the Roman people."[92]

St. Augustine's The City of God

The sack of Rome by Alaric in 410 was the occasion at which Saint Augustine wrote one of the most important Christian works of the last two thousand years, The City of God. The devastation of 410 left the Roman world in a deep state of shock. Those Romans who had not yet become Catholic wondered if the

Roman gods might be punishing the City for abandoning the ancient religion of Roman polytheism. *The City of God* served as Augustine's consolation to the Christian West by explaining that the City of God would prevail regardless of the fortunes of the City of Man.

Augustine's treatment of the sack of Rome returned to the biblical theme of Christians as pilgrims or earthly sojourners longing for a supernatural homeland. Augustine successfully echoed the words of Saint Paul:

> But now they desire a better, that is to say, a heavenly country. Therefore, God is not ashamed to be called their God: for he hath prepared for them a city (Heb 11:16).

Elsewhere, Saint Paul writes: "We have here no lasting city, but we seek the city that is to come" (Heb 13:14). According to Paul, God had prepared a city for Christians, but this city was *not* Rome. This city was not even Jerusalem. Rather, this new city was entirely spiritual and entirely eschatological. The Apostles referred to it as a new and heavenly Jerusalem. Saint Paul encouraged the Hebrew Christians who had been persecuted in earthly Jerusalem to seek the heavenly Jerusalem: "But you have come to Mount Zion and to the city of the living God, the heavenly Jerusalem" (Heb 12:22). In a similar way, Saint John recorded the final destination of the Christian in the holy city which comes down from above: "And I saw the holy city, the New Jerusalem, coming down out of heaven from God, prepared as a bride adorned for her husband" (Apoc 21:2).

Jerusalem vs. Hierosolym

For the Christians of the first century, a subtle distinction in spelling illustrated the difference between the earthly Jerusalem of the Jews and the spiritual Jerusalem of the Christians. If you read the Greek New Testament or the Latin Vulgate, you may have noticed various spellings of the word Jerusalem.

In the Greek New Testament, Jerusalem is spelled in two ways. One version is spelled with the letter 'y' reading *Hierosolym*. The other version is the familiar *Jerusalem*. The two forms are also preserved in the Latin Vulgate version of the New Testament. Also, in some of the deuterocánonical books in the Septuagint and Vulgate, you'll see *Hierosolym*. *Jerusalem* is the more ancient form. *Hierosolym* is a later form influenced by the Greek language.

The Greek word *Hierosolyma* includes the Greek root for sacred cultic words. Hiereus is priest. Hieron is temple. The Greek writers made a Greek play-on-words to denote Jerusalem as a Hierosolym—a "temple" city. The New Testament seems to use both forms, but employs Hierosolym as the physical "temple city" in Judaea, but Jerusalem assumes a spiritual significance. In Christian literature, Hierosolym is slightly polemical. Jerusalem, on the other hand, can refer to Heaven itself.

Saint Paul, in Galatians, refers to meeting Peter in geographical Hierosolym (Gal 1:17); however, in the same epistle he uses Jerusalem when referring to "that Jerusalem which is above is free, which is our mother" (Gal 4:26). Likewise, Saint John uses only Hierosolym in his Gospel (thirteen times), and he uses only Jerusalem in the Apocalypse (three times). In his Apocalypse, Jerusalem always refers to the Holy City, which is Heaven. Here we find a subtle reminder that the earthly city of the Jews is not the promised city of God. Rather, the celestial City of God is the true Jerusalem to which we are called.

Saint Paul reminded the Hebrew Christians in the first century that Christ reigned from the heavenly Jerusalem, not the earthly Jerusalem. So also did Saint

Augustine remind the Roman Christians that Rome itself was not the celestial City of God. Rome was divinely chosen by God to be the mother and mistress of all true Churches of Christ. Nevertheless, God did not decree the political or temporal security of Rome. Rome is a means. Heaven is the final end.

For Saint Augustine, human history is the battle between two cities, the City of God against the City of Man. Our future hope lies not with political citizenship within the secular City of Man, but with citizenship within the celestial City of God. The sack of Rome in 410 revealed that God would protect the Roman Catholic Church, but that the city itself was not heaven on earth.

Saint Augustine believed that Rome held a place of preeminence by virtue of the martyrdom of Saints Peter and Paul, and God used Rome to extend the City of God, not the City of Man. Augustine clearly believed in the preeminence of Peter as the chief of the Apostles and Bishop of Rome. Authority derived from the Rome of Peter, and not from Rome of the Caesars. In a certain sense, Augustine's message was ultimately confirmed by the peculiar esteem that Alaric held for the Basilica of Saint Peter. When all of Rome was burned and plundered, only the Vatican basilica housing the relics of Saint Peter remained unharmed. This serves as a memorial that the political calamities affecting the secular state can never destroy the one true Church built on Saint Peter, the Rock of God.

Augustine's *City of God* also highlights that fact that the Catholic Church cannot be bound to the fate of any nation. Despite Constantine's designation of Christianity as the official religion of the Roman Empire, Augustine recognized that the Empire could never be the Church. The Roman Church employed the Roman Empire in her evangelization, but the Roman Church could not become the Roman Empire. Conversely, the Roman

Empire cannot become the Roman Church. Truly Roman Christianity should be oriented toward the heavenly New Jerusalem. Even when the Emperor is Catholic, Augustine's doctrine confirms the teaching of Christ: "Render therefore to Caesar the things that are Caesar's, and to God the things that are God's" (Mt 22:1). The Byzantine error of *caesaropapism*—the false doctrine that the Caesar can act as the Pope—is ultimately a confusion of this Augustinian principle. The Empire cannot serve as the Church. The Emperor cannot serve as the Pope.

Augustine's *City of God* is a sober rethinking of the political optimism of the Christians following the immediate conversion of Constantine. Those Christians went from being severely persecuted by the Roman Empire on one day to being honored and subsidized by the Roman Empire on the next. Understandably, these Christians were eager to see the Roman Empire as indistinguishable from the Roman Church. The destruction of Rome less than one hundred years later reminded these Christians that Rome was not the *goal* of evangelization but a *means* to evangelization. The story of Christendom had only just begun.

This is an important lesson for contemporary Catholics wrestling with the secular powers of our day. Catholics will never be successful in instituting heaven on earth. This does not mean that we should not strive to fulfill our Savior's prayer, "thy kingdom come thy will be done, on earth as it is in heaven." Rather, we must recognize that it is the Catholic Church herself who is the divinely appointed means of salvation, restoration, and renovation. The temporal principalities will always remain Cities of Man to the extent that sin reigns on earth.

The City of God remains in heaven but breaks through on earth as Pope Pius XI described in his encyclical on Christ the King in 1925 to commemorate

1600 anniversary of Constantine's Council of Nicea in 325. The important and subtle distinction regarding the Church and the State is that the City of God works through the City of Man but is not identical to it. An analogy makes this clear. God can use humans and He can work through them to bring about His will. Yet, God's cooperation with men does not entail that all their acts are His acts. Similarly, God has chosen Rome as a human empire so as to bring about the evangelization of the Gentiles. This does not entail that Rome itself is entitled to special treatment or special protection. When God draws away His protective hand from Rome, Augustine argues, that does not signal His rejection of Christian Rome. Rather, it reminds His people that their home is not here. "Our commonwealth is in heaven, and from it we await a Savior, the Lord Jesus Christ" (Phil 3:20).

Is Rome Now Irrelevant?

After contemplating the political demise of Rome, Constantine's creation of a so-called "New Rome" at Constantinople, and the Augustinian idea of an ideal "City of God" in Heaven, one might ask, "If our true home is Heaven, why is Rome still important?" It would seem that Rome crumbled just as Christianity gained momentum. Could one not argue that God used Rome for his purposes and that the city is now irrelevant to contemporary man?

The title of this book suggests otherwise: *The Eternal City*. Rome will continue to the be the seat of the Vicar of Christ "until the fullness of the Gentiles has come in" (Rom 11:25). The First Vatican Council (A.D. 1870) taught that the "Holy Roman See was founded and consecrated with Blessed Peter's blood."[93] It is surprising to read here that Peter, a mere man, consecrated the city of Rome with his blood. No doubt, it was in virtue of his office as the Vicar and Representative of Christ that Peter was able to consecrate a city to God. Now this consecration was not merely for a limited era of time. Rather, the consecration was perpetual. The First Vatican Council also taught that the Vicar of Christ and Successor of Peter is the *Roman* Pontiff by divinely instituted law, and that this office is perpetual until the end of time:

> Therefore, if anyone says that it is not by the institution of Christ the Lord himself (that is to say, by divine law) that Blessed Peter should have perpetual successors in the primacy over the whole Church; or that the Roman Pontiff is not the successor of blessed Peter in this primacy: let him be anathema.[94]

Christ's establishment of Rome as the perpetual Apostolic See is not intended as a legalistic mechanism to limit salvation throughout the earth. Moreover, it is certainly not meant to restrict grace. Rather, Rome was established as the perpetual Apostolic See so that full communion might be achieved among Christians, as the First Vatican Council explained:

> For this reason it has always been necessary for every Church—that is to say the faithful throughout the world—to be in agreement with the Roman Church because of its more effective leadership. In consequence of being joined, as members to head, with that See, from which the rights of sacred communion flow to all, they will grow together into the structure of a single body.[95]

So while our supernatural goal is the beatific vision of Heaven, there is a practical need for an earthly capital so that the life of the Most Holy Trinity might be shared on earth—so that sacred communion might flow to all. As Saint Thomas Aquinas taught, grace perfects nature. The heavenly City of God maintains Rome as God's temporal colony on earth. While the city of Rome is not our final home, she remains the divinely appointed city from which the perpetual Vicars of Christ teach, govern, and sanctify. As Daniel foretold, this kingdom shall be an everlasting kingdom (Dan 7:26-27).

NOTES

[89] Saint Jerome, *Epistle* 126.

[90] Jaroslav Pelikan, *The Excellent Empire: The Fall of Rome and the Triumph of the Church* (San Francisco: Harper & Row Publishers, 1987) p. 15. Pelikan's use of the phrase "the social triumph of the Ancient Church" is derived from the title of a book by Shirley Jackson Case, *The Social Triumph of the Ancient Church* (New York: Harper & Brothers, 1933).

[91] Jerome, *Epistles* 46:12. Marcella did not flee Rome and instead received a martyr's death when Alaric seized the city in 410.

[92] Edward Gibbon, *The History of the Decline and Fall of the Roman Empire*, ed. J.B. Bury, 7 vols. London: Methuen, 1896-1900). Vol. III, p. 323.

[93] First Vatican Council, Session 4, Chapter 2, 2.

[94] First Vatican Council, Session 4, Chapter 2, 5.

[95] First Vatican Council, Session 4, Chapter 2, 4.

CONCLUSION:
CHRIST'S ROMAN CHURCH

This brings an end to the *Catholic Origins of Catholicism* Trilogy. The first volume *The Crucified Rabbi* sought to demonstrate that Christ and His Catholic Church are the perfect fulfillment of over three hundred Old Testament Jewish prophecies. *The Crucified Rabbi* was a book about how Catholicism rose out of Judaism. This third volume *The Eternal City* is a book about how Catholicism rose from within pagan Rome. The first book was one about Jews. This last book was about Gentiles.

The middle book *The Catholic Perspective on Paul* was a book of mediation standing between the Jews on one hand and the Gentiles on the other. How is it that the redemption of Christ apples to both Jews and Gentiles? What is the nature of the universal Church and her sacraments? These important questions are answered by Saint Paul.

Of the three books, I believe that *The Eternal City* is the most important. We live in an age of misguided ecumenism in which every well-intended idea and religion must be not only tolerated but celebrated. To the extent, then, that the Catholic Church ignores her Roman identity, she forgets her ancient nobility. Our claim that the Church is Roman affirms her connection to the historic Christ who was born under Augustus Caesar and crucified under Pontius Pilate. To affirm that the Church is Roman is to magnify the mercy of

Christ who did not leave us as orphans but sent the Holy Spirit to guide the Popes reigning from the city of Rome. The Roman identity of the Catholic Church reveals that she is unique, not only among all the religions of earth, but especially among the various Christian denominations with their contradictory doctrines.

Regrettably, many Catholics today have never heard of the great war of God's saints echoing in the prophecies of Daniel, proclaimed by the preaching of the Son of Man, and illustrated in that last battle against the Beast of the Apocalypse. The Christ that defeats Daniel's Rome is not a soft and effeminate sage. Rather, He is the conquering King of Kings and Lord of Lords.

The spiritual imperialism of Christ was fully appreciated by our Christian forefathers. We, however, have forgotten the ancient feats of strength demonstrated by the monastics of old. For example, the penance of the Desert Fathers would have brought a sense of wonder even to the Roman Stoic Cato. We have forgotten the triumphant Roman martyrs, such as Saint Lawrence who would have kindled awe in the bravest Roman pagan warriors, such as Mucius Scaevolus. As the baptized have forgotten the noble army of martyrs that once fertilized the Eternal City with faith, so also have they lost esteem for Rome's spiritual dignity.

As the world forgot Rome, they forgot Christ our Savior. They spurned the virginal embrace of Holy Mother Church. In exchange, they embraced the Great Harlot and her Beast described in the seventeenth chapter of the Apocalypse. Roman history, then, is essentially a story of two women. One woman is the Harlot of Babylon seduced by paganism, idolatry, and self-love. The other is a Virgin and Mother infused with faith, hope, and divine charity. We must not confuse the one with the other.

What could be more abhorrent to the heretics of our age than the dignified orthodoxy of Rome? The heretics have never been able to tolerate the majesty of Rome. Among the ranks of Luther, Calvin, Zwingli, and Cranmer the very word *Romanist* became a vile and pejorative slur against those that preserved the Apostolic Faith of Rome. Blessed John Henry Newman noted that those in history who employed the term "Romanist" as a curse word were always and everywhere heretics.

The defenders of modernism, neo-paganism, carnal immorality, inclusive language, and effeminate liturgy simply cannot tolerate the thought that Christ the King assumed the Roman court as His own. The Christ of the Apocalypse, slaying the heathen Roman beast and its harlot, is not politically correct. They dislike the fact that the Vicar of Christ reigns over the Church from the imperial capital of Rome. In their jihad for tolerance, they cannot tolerate the reality that the tabernacle is the hushed abode of His rule over the earth. This is why they mock the Pope. This is why they relocate His tabernacle away from the center of Christ's liturgical court. The true Emperor of Heaven must be dethroned—symbolically by showing disregard of the Supreme Pontiff; and truly by showing dishonor to the Blessed Sacrament.

The enemies of Christ resent the fact that Holy Mother Church still speaks to her children chiefly in Latin—a language that has died but risen again. Latin is still the language of the household of faith. As C.S. Lewis once allegorized in his *Pilgrim's Regress*, Mother Church always speaks tenderly to her children, albeit she speaks to them in Latin. She takes what is old and makes all things new. The liturgy and magisterial teachings of the Church are still published *in Latin*. The enemies of Christ ignore that while Hebrew and Greek, the languages of the Old and New Testaments, were inscribed over the sacred head of Christ, so also was Latin: *Jesus Nazarenus Rex Judaeorum.*

The New Evangelization initiated by Pope Blessed John Paul II during the great Jubilee Year of A.D. 2000 must recall the Old Evangelization successfully extended by the ancient Bishops of Rome over the pagan tribes of Europe. Apostolic Succession from that age ensures Apostolic success in this age. Europe was not won over to the banner of Christ by undermining the centrality of Rome. Rather, Rome was the standard bearer for Christ. Rome brought civility, nobility, order, and most importantly, she brought salvation. This is to say that *Roman* Catholicism is not an incidental preference. *Roman* Catholicism is absolutely essential for human redemption. If our Byzantine friends murmur, let them merely consult their own history. Whenever the Eastern churches affirmed their connection with the Rome of Saint Peter, orthodoxy reigned and evangelical missions expanded. Whenever the East disregarded Rome, heresy spread and missionary work lost traction.

Christianity is *the* religion rooted in human history since it holds that God entered history as a man. The historical fact, then, that Jesus Christ was born and died under the Roman imperial standard is not an accident of history. Christ's redemptive activity under Caesar was the explicit desire and plan of God established before the very foundation of creation. Before God created Adam and Eve, He knew that His Son would die on a Roman cross, and also that He would rise again to conquer the Roman Empire. The eternal plan of God was fulfilled only when the Jewish Messiah came crashing up against Rome of the Gentiles. The Jewish Messiah won, and He gathered His spoils. *Deo gratias.*

AD MAJOREM DEI GLORIAM
SANCTA MARIA DEI GENETRIX, ORA PRO NOBIS
SANCTE PETRE ET SANCTE PAULE, ORA PRO NOBIS

APPENDIX A: TIME LINE OF ROMAN HISTORY

586 B.C.	Babylonians destroy the Temple in Jerusalem and deport Jews
456 B.C.	Ezra sent to Jerusalem to rebuild the Temple
167 B.C.	Antiochus IV desecrates the Temple in Jerusalem
164 B.C.	The Maccabees re-consecrate the Temple in Jerusalem
161 B.C.	Jerusalem enters political alliance with Rome
160 B.C.	Judah Maccabeus dies
63 B.C.	Judea loses independence and falls under Roman rule
44 B.C.	Julius Caesar assassinated
37 B.C.	Herod the Great appointed ruler of Judea
27 B.C.	Octavian becomes sole Emperor of Rome and Caesar Augustus
1 B.C.	December 25. Christ born.
A.D. 1	January 1. Christ circumcised.
A.D. 26	Pontius Pilate appointed governor of Judea
30	Baptism of Christ
33	Crucifixion and resurrection of Christ
36	Conversion and baptism of Paul
41	Herod Agrippa ascends throne

42	Martyrdom of James the Greater, Apostles flee Jerusalem
	Traditional date for Peter's first visit to Rome[96]
44	Herod Agrippa dies
49	Edict of Claudius banishes all Jews from Rome, Peter goes to Antioch
50	Council at Jerusalem (Acts 15)
55	Claudius dies
56	Edict of Claudius repealed, Jews return to Rome, Peter returns to Rome
57	Paul writes *Romans* to address the growing tension arising between Jewish and Gentile Christians after the great immigration of Jewish Christians to the Rome in A.D. 56 after the repeal of the Edict of Claudius.
58	Paul imprisoned at Caesarea
59	Paul transferred from Caesarea (August)
60	Paul arrives in Rome
64	Great Fire of Rome; Neronian persecution begins
67	Traditional date for the martyrdom of Peter and Paul (29 June)
69	Year of the Four Emperors (Galba, Otho, Vitellius, and Vespasian)
70	Titus Flavius and his Roman legions sack Jerusalem and destroy the Temple
202-210	Persecution by Emperor Septimus Severus (Martyrs Perpetua & Felicity)
250-251	Persecution by Emperor Decius (Martyrs Pope Pontian & Hippolytus)
253-260	Persecution by Emperor Valerian (Martyrs Pope Sixtus II, Laurence, Cyprian)
303	Roman Emperor Diocletian issues his first *Edict against the Christians* (24 Feb)

306	Constantine hailed as Augustus by his troops at York, England
312	Constantine defeated Maxentius at the Battle of Milvian Bridge
313	Constantine and Licinius issue the *Edict of Milan* granting tolerance to Christianity
324	Constantine announces that Byzantium will become "New Rome"
325	Council of Nicaea condemns Arian heresy
330	Byzantium officially becomes the capital of the Roman Empire
337	Constantine is baptized and dies shortly afterward (22 May); Byzantium is renamed *Constantinople* ("City of Constantine")
361-363	Emperor Julian the Apostate reverts back to the pagan gods of old Rome
380	Roman Emperor Theodosius declares the Catholic Church as the official religion of the Roman Empire.

NOTES

[96] See Arthur Stapylton Barnes, *Christianity at Rome in the Apostolic Age* (Westport, Connecticut: Greenwood Press, 1971), pp. 2-13. Barnes provides an argument in support of the claim found in the *Liber Pontificales* stating that twenty-five years elapsed from Peter's first arrival in Rome to his martyrdom in Rome, i.e. A.D. 42-67.

APPENDIX B: DATES OF DANIEL'S FOUR KINGDOMS

THERE ARE ESSENTIALLY two different perspectives with respect to the date of the Book of Daniel: the sixth century B.C. date and the second century B.C. date. According to tradition, the book of Daniel is a prophetic work composed by its namesake shortly after the Babylonian captivity in the sixth century B.C. In the Christian Bible, the book of Daniel is the fourth of the "major prophets" after Isaiah, Jeremiah, and Ezekiel. However, in the Hebrew Bible, the book of Daniel is not collected among the *Neviim* ("Prophets") but among the *Ketuvim* ("Writings"), after Esther and before Ezra. The reason for this is that the book of Daniel did not reach its final form until *after* the section of the *Neviim* ("Prophets") had been finalized and "closed."

The book of Daniel in its final Catholic form is composed in Hebrew and Aramaic. The later deuterocanonical passages (Dan 3:1-68; chapter 13; chapter 14) are only known in Greek and Latin versions of the book, though they might very likely have come from a Hebrew/Aramaic source. All this is to say that the book of Daniel seems to be a collection of writings. There are three basic divisions:

1. The third person account of Daniel in the Court of Babylon (chs. 1-6)

2. The first person account of Daniel's visions
    (chs. 7-12)

3. Deuterocanonical additions to the book (3:1-68;
    chs. 13-14)

Most modern scholars believe that the book of Daniel is
an edited collection of writings that found its final form
some time before 164 B.C. These proponents of the
late-date school prove the 164 B.C. date by citing the
following textual difficulties:

*   historical errors in chronology
*   linguistic evidence of a later, Greek-influenced
    period
*   the precise prophetic fulfillment of prophecies
    prior to 164 B.C. (everything before Daniel
    11:39)
*   and a failed prophecy concerning events after
    164 B.C. (from Daniel 11:39 onward)

The third century Neo-Platonist and anti-Christian
polemicist Porphyry (A.D. 233-304) seems to have been
the first to point out these textual difficulties. Porphyry
noted that the eleventh chapter of Daniel focuses on a
series of battles between the "King of the North" and
the "King of the South," and it is generally recognized
that these visions depict the struggle between the
Seleucid "Kings of the North" and the Ptolemaic
"Kings of the South" after the death of Alexander the
Great in 323 B.C. Porphyry cited this as an example of
ex eventu prophecy or "back-dating" a text so that it
appears to be prophetic.

In order to illustrate how *ex eventu* prophecy might
be created, consider the following example. Suppose
that I desire to make an *ex eventu* prophecy concerning
American history. I would pose myself as a popular

character of the eighteenth century, say Benjamin Franklin. I would then write a mysterious prophecy that claims to be written by Benjamin Franklin and contains historical details particular to his time. I would then go on and write something like this:

Benjamin Franklin recorded these words in the tenth year of His Royal Highness of the Island of Britannia:

I dreamt a dream. I saw a great Eagle arise from the earth. With a loud voice, the Eagle screeched: "Julius the Fourth! Julius the Fourth! Julius the Fourth!"

Then I saw an island emerge from sea. Seated on the island was a pompous tyrant arrayed in red. Let the reader understand. His name EGROEG and his number is three. He bore a sword and tried to slay the Eagle, but he could not. Out of his mouth came lobsters arrayed in red and in their claws they bore muskets. They swam across the sea and crawled onto the beaches of the Freedom Land.

Out of the Freedom Land came valiant men dressed in red, white, and blue. They slew the lobsters arrayed in red, and instead of a throne, they established a tree with three branches.

But in time black-skinned men appeared, also arrayed in red, white, and blue. They were enslaved and so the Freedom Land became rent from east to west. The north became blue and the south became grey.

Four score and seven years later, a man arose in the House called White. The man was tall, and on his head he wore a tall hat. He announced: "They shall be free." But as the tall man sat in the great theatre, he received a mortal wound and was no more. And yet he lived.

The blue of the north became strong and they covered over the grey of the south. And then chains fell from the black skinned men arrayed in red, white, and blue, and they came and bowed at the tomb of the tall man. And so the Freedom Land became truly free.

Let all who read this prophecy of Benjamin Franklin be ready for the great freedom that shall be brought by the Eagle after the earth shall encircle the sun ten times from this year.

Any unwitting reader of this "prophecy" would be amazed at the supernatural foresight of Benjamin Franklin writing all the way back in 1766 (the tenth year of King George III). Franklin foretold the birth of the American nation (symbolized by the Eagle) on Julius the Fourth or the Fourth of July from the tyranny of the British island and George III (EGROEG, whose number is three). The red lobsters are allusions to the coming redcoats of the English army. The Americans who establish the Freedom Land defeated the "lobsters." The tree of three branches refers the reader to our three branches of government – executive, legislative, and judicial. Next, the nation is divided between Union and Confederate forces over the "black skinned men." Abraham Lincoln arrives in the White House (House of White) but dies in a theatre. Nevertheless, the North overcomes the South, and the black-skinned Americans are freed.

According to late-date critics of Daniel, this is akin to how the Book of Daniel was composed – it is an after-the-fact, *ex eventu* prophecy. According to critics, the Book of Daniel is simply a composition penned not long before 164 B.C. by an anonymous Jewish author that relates past events in apocalyptic language and fails at predicting the events surrounding the future death of Antiochus IV.

The traditional date for the Book of Daniel was not again questioned until the rise of the textual criticism in the seventeenth century. As scholars began to doubt the inspiration of the Sacred Scriptures they began to question the prophetic passages of Scriptures. They explained accurate prophecies as *ex eventu* prophecies, that is, prophecies that were "back-dated" only to appear as prophecies of the future.

Most scholars today date the Book of Daniel between the second campaign of Antiochus IV against Egypt in 167 B.C. and the death of Antiochus IV in April 163 B.C. They argue that everything before Daniel 11:39 is historically accurate because that material is merely prophecy "after the fact." When the Book of Daniel actually does make an attempt at real prophecy, the details of the future are "incorrect." After Daniel 11:39, the prophecy "wrongly" describes the death of Antiochus IV in this way:

> He will pitch his royal tents between the seas
> at the beautiful holy mountain. Yet he will
> come to his end, and no one will help him
> (Dan 11:45).

However, Antiochus IV did *not* die in Palestine but in Syria. For most, this "error" proves that the author of Daniel composed the prophecies sometime just before the death of Antiochus IV.

Saint Jerome acknowledged the uncanny historical accuracy of Daniel's visions, but he held to the traditional view that Daniel foretold the details through his gift of prophecy and not by a pseudepigraphal attempt to "back-date" historical events in the form as an alleged prophecy. Daniel "failed" to prophesy the death of Antiochus IV, because Daniel was not foreseeing the death of Antiochus IV but a future Antichrist figure at the end of time. Those who follow the traditional understanding of Saint Jerome assign the protocanonical text of Daniel (chs. 1-12) to a historical prophet named Daniel living in the sixth century B.C.

There are reasons for dating the book of Daniel to the early traditional date in the sixth century. First, Christ regarded the book of Daniel to be by "Daniel the prophet" (Mt 24:15). Secondly, the first century Jewish historian Josephus (ca. A.D. 40-100) wrote, "When the book of Daniel was shown to Alexander the Great (d. 323 B.C.), wherein Daniel declared that one of the Greeks should destroy the empire of the Persians, he supposed that he was the person intended" (*Antiquities of the Jews*, Bk. XI, ch. viii, 5). This would suggest that Daniel had been composed sometime before 323 B.C. Josephus also explains that the Palestinian canon of Scripture was closed by Ezra in the middle of the fifth century B.C., and this canon includes the protocanonical form of Daniel (*Contra Apion*, 8).

Thirdly, the book of 1 Maccabees shows an acquaintance with the Greek version of the book of Daniel (for examples, consult 1 Macc. 1:54, Dan. 9:27; 1 Macc. 2:59-60, Dan. 3:6). This demonstrates that the book of Daniel had already been translated into Greek by the end of the second century B.C., making it nearly impossible for the entire work to have been composed during the reign of Antiochus IV. Fourthly, the Sibylline Oracles (ca. 170 B.C.) contain an allusion to Antiochus IV, and to the ten horns of Dan. 7:7-24 and thus indicate that Daniel had been circulated prior to the date advocated by proponents of the later date.

The dating of the Book of Daniel is crucial to the identity of the four kingdoms. Most biblical scholars assume that Daniel was primarily a treatise against Antiochus IV and therefore conclude that the fourth kingdom must be Greece, using the following enumeration:

First Kingdom	Babylonian Empire
Second Kingdom	Median Empire
Third Kingdom	Persian Empire
Fourth Kingdom	Greek Empire

This enumeration has become almost unanimously received by scholars and can even be found in some Catholic commentaries. This is a regrettable concession, in the author's opinion. However, there is strong evidence against assigning Media and Persia as different world empires in Daniel. The book itself understands "the Medes and the Persians" as one single kingdom that succeeded Babylon (cf. Daniel 5:28). Daniel quotes the king and other rulers as referring to their kingdom as that of "the Medes and the Persians" (cf. Daniel 6:8, 12, 15). The Persian king Cyrus was married to a Mede and possessed both Persian and Median blood. It is also a historical fact that the Medes and the Persians were not two distinct kingdoms when they conquered the Babylonian Empire. Therefore it is anachronistic to divide them into two kingdoms at the time of the decline of the Babylonian empire.

Those who follow the enumeration above neglect the clear fact that the imagery that Daniel provides for the four kingdoms does correspond to characteristics of those kingdoms. The bear with one side raised refers to the uneven composite of the Medes and the Persians. The three ribs stand for the three nations conquered by the Medo-Persian Empire: Babylon, Lydia, and Egypt. The four-headed and four-winged leopard has no referent to the Persians, but history is clear that four generals or "four heads" ruled the united Greek Empire after the death of Alexander the Great. Even if we grant that Daniel was composed just prior to the death of Antiochus IV in 164 B.C., the following enumeration is more likely:

First Kingdom	Babylonian Empire
Second Kingdom	Medo-Persian Empire
Third Kingdom	Greek Empire of Alexander the Great
Fourth Kingdom	Tyrannical Seleucid Empire of Antiochus IV

Whether the author wrote in the sixth or second century B.C. he saw that the fourth kingdom to come was more fragile, divisive, and monstrous than the previous three kingdoms. The Maccabean revolt threw off the yoke of the Greco-Syrian tyranny of the Seleucids once and for all in 164 B.C. Therefore, the tyrannical kingdom had yet to materialize. It awaited the coming of an even fiercer kingdom – the Roman Empire.

I would like to make a final argument regarding the Fourth Kingdom as Rome from the teaching of Christ Himself and that of the New Testament. Jesus Christ, the Apostle Paul, and the Book of Revelation assume that the identity of the Fourth Kingdom is Rome. The apocryphal Apocalypse of Ezra also clearly describes the Roman Empire "as the fourth kingdom which appeared in a vision to your brother Daniel" (4 Esdras 12:11). This does not pose a problem for Christians because the prophets are often reinterpreted so that their words speak of a series of interconnected events with multiple fulfillments. The historical context of the prophets does not necessarily provide the proper interpretation of a passage. Take for example Hosea 1:11, that states, "Out of Egypt I have called my Son." This originally referred to the Lord's deliverance of Israel from Egypt under Moses. But it was also prophetic of the Holy Family's descent and ascent from Egypt (cf. Matthew 2:15). Isaiah prophesied that "a virgin shall conceive and bear a son, and shall call his name Immanuel" (Isaiah 7:14). This had a fulfillment in Isaiah's day, but its ultimate fulfillment is found in the Virgin Birth of Christ (Mt 1:23).

Regardless of the Book of Daniel's original historical context, Christ and His Apostles interpreted its prophecies as being fulfilled in their own century. Christ declared Himself to be the Danielic *Son of Man* on a number of occasions (Dan 7:13; Mt 27:64; Mk 8:31; 14:62). For Christ, the role of the Son of Man was not a past event associated with the Maccabean revolt but a current reality. Daniel presents this Son of Man as the mediator of Israel's salvation and received kingdom (Dan 7:13; Mt 12:28). According to Daniel, the manifestation of the Son of Man occurs in the era of the Fourth Kingdom, and Christian belief firmly holds that Christ lived, died, and rose again under Roman rule.

Moreover, it is clear that Christ understood the Fourth Kingdom to be the dominant secular power of His day – Rome. This is clear because Christ foresees Daniel's "desolating sacrilege" or "abomination of desolation" as occurring in the near future and upon "this generation" (Mt 23:36; 24:15, 34; Mk 13:14; Lk 21:20). This also confirms that Christ perceived the Fourth Kingdom of Daniel as the Roman Empire since it was the Romans who desecrated the Temple and destroyed Jerusalem in A.D. 70, exactly within "this generation" of Christ's public ministry. Saint Paul's identification of the "man of sin" and the allusions to Rome in the Book of Revelation further confirm that early Christians strongly believed that they were living in the era of Daniel's monstrous Fourth Kingdom.

The Christian is in no place to say that Christ was wrong in His identification of Daniel's Fourth Kingdom with the Roman Empire. The Son of God clearly taught that Daniel's description of the Son of Man and abomination of desolation applied to His own ministry and the close of the Old Covenant era. While it is possible that the Book of Daniel is primarily concerned with persecution under the Greek Empire, the ultimate fulfillment of the book is found in Christ's role as the Son of Man and the coming Roman desecration of Jerusalem in A.D. 70. Therefore, the Roman Catholic Church has always held that the Fourth Kingdom of Daniel is ultimately the Roman Empire because Christ interprets the passage in such a manner.

BIBLIOGRAPHY

A Concise Hebrew and Aramaic Lexicon of the Old Testament.
William L. Holladay, ed. Grand Rapids, Michigan:
William B. Eerdmans Publishing, 1988.

Alter, Robert. *Genesis: Translation and Commentary.* New
York: W. W. Norton & Company, 1996.

*Anastasii Bibliothecarii Historia, de vitis romanorum pontificum
a b. Petro apostolo usque ad Nicolaum I nunquam
hactenus typis excusa. Deinde Vita Hadriani II et
Stephani VI.* 1602 Editio Princeps.

Aquinas, Thomas. *Summa Theologica.* Translated by
Fathers of the English Dominican Province.
Notre Dame, IN: Christian Classics, Ave Maria
Press, 1981 [1948].

The Babylonian Talmud. I. Epstein, ed. London: Soncino
Press, 1935-38.

Barnes, Arthur Stapylton. *Christianity at Rome in the
Apostolic Age: An Attempt at Reconstruction of
History.* Westport, Connecticut: Greenwood
Press, 1938.

Biblia Hebraica Stuttgartensia. K. Elliger and W. Rudolph,
eds. Stuttgart: Deutche Bibelgesellschaft, Fourth
Corrected Edition, 1990.

Brown, Peter. *The Cult of the Saints: Its Rise and Function in
Latin Christianity.* Chicago: University of Chicago
Press, 1981.

Catechism of the Catholic Church. Second ed. Vatican City:
Libreria Editrice Vaticana, 1997.

Catholic Encyclopedia. New York: Robert Appleton
Company, 1913.

Chronicles – Maccabees: The Navarre Bible Commentary. Jose Maria Casciaro, ed. New York: Scepter Publishers, 2003.

Codex Iuris Canonici. Vatican City: Libreria Editrice Vaticana, 1983.

de Nanteuil, Hugues. *The Dates of the Birth and Death of Jesus Christ.* Translated by J.S. Daly and F. Egregyi. France: Tradibooks, 2008.

Dillard, Raymond B. & Tremper Longman, III. *An Introduction to the Old Testament.* Grand Rapids, Michigan: Zondervan Publishing House, 1993.

Eusebius. *Life of Constantine.* Translated by Averil Cameron and Stuart G. Hall. Oxford: Clarendon Press, 1999.

Gibbon, Edward. *The History of the Decline and Fall of the Roman Empire.* 7 Volumes. Edited by J.B. Bury. London: Methuen, 1896-1900.

Grant, Michael. *Constantine the Great.* New York: Charles Scribner's Sons, 1994.

Guarducci, Margherita. *The Tomb of Saint Peter: The New Discoveries in the Sacred Grottoes of the Vatican.* New York: Hawthorn Books, 1960.

Johnson, M. D. *The Purpose of Biblical Genealogies.* New York: Cambridge, 1969.

Josephus, Flavius. *Jewish Antiquities: Books I-III.* Loeb Classical Library No. 242. Trans. H. St. John Thackeray. Cambridge, MA: Harvard University Press, 1997.

_____. *The Works of Josephus: New Updated Edition.* Trans. William Whiston. Peabody, MA: Hendrickson Publishers, 1987.

Kelly, J.N.D. *The Oxford Dictionary of Popes.* Oxford: University Press, 1986.

Kirschbaum, Engelbert. *The Tombs of St. Peter and St. Paul.* New York: St. Martin's Press, 1959.

Leithart, Peter. *The Kingdom and the Power.* Phillipsburg, NJ: Presbyterian and Reformed Publishing, 1993.

Levering, Matthew. *Christ's Fulfillment of Torah and Temple: Salvation according to Thomas Aquinas.* Notre Dame, Indiana: University of Notre Dame Press, 2002.

Liber Pontificalis. Merchantville, NJ: Evolution Publishing, 1916 reprint.

Lightfoot, J.B. *The Apostolic Fathers.* London: Macmillan, 1890.

LXX Septuaginta. Alfred Ralfs, ed. Stuttgart: Wurttembergische Bebelanstalt/Deutsche Bibelgesellschaft, 1935.

Maimonides. *The Code of Maimonides (Mishneh Torah).* Translated by Abraham Hershman. New Haven: Yale University Press, 1949.

Martyrologium Romanum. Libreria Editrice Vaticana, 2001.

Mazar, Amihai. *Archaeology of the Land of the Bible: 10,000-586 B.C.* New York: Doubleday, 1992.

Meagher, James L. *How Christ Said the First Mass.* Rockford, Illinois: TAN Books, 1984.

The Oxford Dictionary of the Christian Church. F. L. Cross, ed. New York: Oxford University Press, 1997.

Pelikan, Jaroslav. *The Emergence of the Catholic Tradition (100-600).* Chicago: University of Chicago Press, 1971.

_____. *The Excellent Empire: The Fall of Rome and the Triumph of the Church.* San Francisco: Harper & Row Publishers, 1987.

Perowne, Stewart, *Caesars and Saints: The Evolution of the Christian State 180-313 A.D.* New York: W. W. Norton & Company, 1962.

Philo Judaeus. *The Works of Philo: Complete and Unabridged, New Updated Edition.* Trans. C. D. Yonge. Peabody, Massachusetts: Hendrickson Publishers, 1993.

Pitre, Brant. *Jesus, the Tribulation, and the End of the Exile.* Grand Rapids: Baker Academic, 2006.

Ratzinger, Joseph. *Eschatology.* Washington, D.C.: Catholic University of America Press, 1988.

Sheed, Frank. *To Know Christ Jesus*. San Francisco: Ignatius Press, 1992.

Shoeman, Roy H. *Salvation is from the Jews: The Role of Judaism in Salvation History from Abraham to the Second Coming*. San Francisco: Ignatius Press, 2003.

Suetonius. *The Lives of the Twelve Caesars*. New York: Random House, 1931.

Tacitus, Cornelius. *Annales IV*. Translated by D.C.A. Shotter. Warminister: Aris & Philips Ltd., 1989.

Telushkin, Joseph. *Jewish Literacy*. New York: William Morrow, 2002.

Vos, Gerhardus. *Biblical Theology: Old and New Testaments*. Carlisle, Pennsylvania: Banner of Truth Trust, 1996.

Walsh, John Evangelist. *The Bones of Saint Peter: The First Full Account of the Search for the Apostle's Body*. New York: Doubleday, 1982.

Walsh, John Evangelist. *The Bones of St. Peter*. New York: Doubleday, 1982.

Ward-Perkins, Bryan. *The Fall of Rome and the End of Civilization*. New York: Oxford University Press, 2005.

Weingreen, J. *A Practical Grammar for Classical Hebrew*. New York: Oxford University Press, 1959.

Wright, N. T. *Climax of the Covenant*. Minneapolis: Augsburg Fortress Publishers, 1993.

_____. *The Resurrection of the Son of God*. Minneapolis: Augsburg Fortress Publishers, 2003.

INDEX

ABOUT TAYLOR MARSHALL

Dr. Taylor Marshall is the Founder of the New Saint Thomas Institute (newsaintthomas.com), a school providing training in the philosophy and theology of Saint Thomas Aquinas. Taylor holds a Ph.D. in Philosophy from the University of Dallas focusing on the Natural Law theory of Saint Thomas Aquinas. He is a graduate of Texas A&M University (BA, Philosophy) Westminster Theological Seminary (MAR, Systematic Theology), and the University of Dallas (MA, Philosophy).

Taylor Marshall was an Episcopal priest in Fort Worth, Texas before being received with his family into the Catholic Church by Bishop Kevin Vann of Fort Worth in 2006. He subsequently served as the Assistant Director of the Catholic Information Center in Washington, D.C., located three blocks north of the White House, where he lectured regularly. He runs a popular Catholic blog on Catholic theology, philosophy, and culture at taylormarshall.com. He is also the author of *The Crucified Rabbi – Judaism and the Origins of Catholic Christianity* and *The Catholic Perspective on Paul – Paul and the Origins of Catholic Christianity*.

Taylor and his wife Joy live in Dallas, Texas with their seven children. He can be contacted at:

taylor@taylormarshall.com

Please visit his blog online at:

www.TaylorMarshall.com

Please review *The Eternal City* at amazon.com!